A DAY IN "THE HOLE"

A DAY IN "THE HOLE"

Risk, Loss, and Excess in
Downtown Lima

✻

Daniella Gandolfo

The University of Chicago Press
Chicago and London

The University of Chicago Press, Chicago 60637
The University of Chicago Press, Ltd., London
© 2025 by The University of Chicago
Published 2025

34 33 32 31 30 29 28 27 26 25   1 2 3 4 5

ISBN-13: 978-0-226-84337-7 (cloth)
ISBN-13: 978-0-226-84339-1 (paper)
ISBN-13: 978-0-226-84338-4 (ebook)
DOI: https://doi.org/10.7208/chicago/9780226843384.001.0001

Library of Congress Cataloging-in-Publication Data

Names: Gandolfo, Daniella author
Title: A day in "The Hole" : risk, loss, and excess in downtown
Lima / Daniella Gandolfo.
Description: Chicago ; London : The University of Chicago Press,
2025. | Includes bibliographical references and index.
Identifiers: LCCN 2025020256 | ISBN 9780226843377 cloth |
ISBN 9780226843391 paperback | ISBN 9780226843384 ebook
Subjects: LCSH: Centro comercial "El Hueco" (Lima, Peru) | Mesa
Redonda (Market : Lima, Peru) | Markets—Peru—Lima | Street
vendors—Peru—Lima—Social conditions | Commerce—Social
aspects—Peru—Lima | Retail trade—Social aspects—Peru—
Lima | Informal sector (Economics)—Peru—Lima |
Lima (Peru)—Economic conditions
Classification: LCC HF5475.P42 L54 2025 | DDC
381.0985/252—dc23/eng/20250715
LC record available at https://lccn.loc.gov/2025020256

Authorized Representative for EU General Product Safety
Regulation (GPSR) queries: **Easy Access System Europe**—
Mustamäe tee 50, 10621 Tallinn, Estonia,
gpsr.requests@easproject.com
Any other queries: https://press.uchicago.edu/press/contact.html

Contents

Preface

A VISION OF EXCESS IN LIMA

I am on my way to El Hueco the morning an article about the infamous market appears online. The Metropolitano bus is flying toward downtown, the haphazardly planned landscape of the city flitting past, and I read on my phone's screen, "Did You Know That Two 'Twin Towers' Were Going to be Built in Lima, but El Hueco Was Left in Their Place?" The reporter states that downtown Lima almost had buildings much like the iconic New York City skyscrapers, but the project was never completed. Below the headline is a montage of the now-disappeared Twin Towers and a digital rendering of the two Lima buildings, which were envisioned in the 1950s for the intersection of Avenidas Abancay and Nicolás de Piérola.

I regularly come across versions of this newspaper story in the city's dailies. They rehash the same details about El Hueco, only some of which are accurate. To begin with, the projected mid-century-style buildings, designed to house government offices, looked nothing like the Twin Towers. But it is true that the plan was truncated. Only one building was finished. The other one, intended to reside across Abancay like a mirror reflection of the first, didn't get past the foundation pit, which remained an abandoned crater for four decades. Not only did one of the anticipated two tallest buildings in Lima fail to materialize but also a huge hole was left in its place. With time, the barren hollow came to be known as "Hueco de Abancay" until a group of law-defying but savvy street vendors, in a widely condemned move, settled into it.

I scroll down to the bottom of the article, and it is exactly what I expect. Its tenor abruptly changes from that of a critical report about a botched state modernization effort to one that rings of fascination and pleasure: The foundation pit inexplicably deserted and the vendors already encroaching on the space, the author moves on to list the "ample variety" of goods now offered at the market—shoes, clothes and accessories, CDs and DVDs, and all manner of other wares that, she says, are of interest to the public. She doesn't mention the contraband, the piracy of copyrighted material, or the brand forging. I instantly relate to the narrative arc typical of these pieces of newspaper trivia, starting with the curious history of the market's location and ending with an enthusiastic appeal and directions for how to get there. As I travel straphanging in the aisle of the bus, I don't doubt that my interest in El Hueco as an anthropologist aligns with my quiet but excited deliberations about which knock-off Caterpillar bag I will buy today.

At the Javier Prado stop, an elderly woman enters carrying a big bundle. Other women harass a young man sitting in one of the red seats reserved for the old and infirm to relinquish his seat. I get the feeling that she and I are bound for the same destination. I picture her unfurling her load and taking over a piece of sidewalk on Abancay or in Mesa Redonda, a cluster of colonial-era city blocks next to El Hueco that is fully dedicated to retail. It strikes me how the idea of invasion—of vendors' incursions onto sidewalks, plazas, city roads, and plain, empty space—is intimately linked to the general perception of poorly regulated worlds like El Hueco and Mesa Redonda. The article I just read suggests—and others like it state outright—that in 1997 the vendors of El Hueco forcibly took over the hole after being evicted from streets that they had invaded before. But this is wrong. El Hueco's vendors owned the property when they moved in, even if this fact was contested for ten years in the courts. The assumption of an invasion, however, takes me back to the mid-1980s when I first became aware of the predominance in Lima of techniques of livelihood that evaded most regulations and the law. Seizure of state and private land for housing and of public spaces for trading was key among those techniques, expressing, like no urban planner or government official ever could, the new value and meaning of urban space.

At Estación Central, the elderly woman and I find ourselves in the same cue of people waiting to catch a connection to Estación La Colmena. But once we are off the bus and walking in the direction of

El Hueco, I quickly pass and leave her behind. The sidewalks are increasingly populated with food and fresh juice carts and tarps with all sorts of goods. There are soaps for sale as well as cotton T-shirts and hardware parts. A few of these small-scale vendors have city permits, but most do not, and all sell their wares without giving out receipts. Down the road, more established commercial venues operate without a license, and elsewhere in the city, clothing and shoe manufacturing shops do without a proper payroll while families build homes without authorization on insecurely occupied land. For at least eighty years, one of the main jobs of city officials and planners in Lima has been to play catch up. One can think of the totality of trading, producing, and building in this way as an underground or shadow economy. But there is nothing underground or in the shadows about the defiant, in-your-face bypassing of legal norms here. The term used to refer to these ways of making a living—which has also been deemed inadequate but has, nevertheless, stuck in Lima since the mid-1980s—is *informality*. It is said to account for 78 percent of businesses and over 62 percent of the labor force in the city, nearly half of which works in commerce.

The first time I encountered the term informality it was used to convey a pragmatic attitude toward making a living. In the face of overly complicated, expensive, and corrupt laws, people disregarded them by, for example, neglecting to apply for permits required to sell children's toys, open a textiles factory, or build a home. This conduct grew out of a perfectly rational calculation and was a sign of the inadequacy not of people or their actions but of laws and institutions. It was also an affirmation of Peruvians' free-market spirit, a people's capitalism piercing through the barriers of a state apparatus that was rotten to the core since colonial times. A couple of years later, I came across an alternative to this lift-oneself-by-the-bootstraps interpretation. Such a massive evasion of regulations was rather a defiant response to a system that privileged those already well-off. The open scorn of the system's norms, as we see to this day in thoroughfares such as Abancay, was a form of rebellion. Means and ends did not so easily fit in the legal or illegal categories because the overhauling of society meant that even morality was in the balance. Both of these views—the first a libertarian, the second a leftist one—were, in part, a reaction to an older theory that viewed the urban poor as a mass of people marginalized by a capitalist economy that kept it on the sidelines. The instant I first stepped into El Hueco and Mesa Redonda, it became clear to me that none of these explanations were entirely suitable.

The one modernist tower that did rise finally comes into view. It is no skyscraper, but it looms over its surroundings. The front entrance and atrium are gated and locked. They are stylized and aloof. The side wings, by contrast, are lackluster and worn down. People gather by the doors, morosely waiting to enter and run some bureaucratic errand. These dingy offices and the tower's area of influence along Abancay have all the marks of Lima's troubled aspirations to become a planned, modern city. The surroundings impress one as improvised and a place where people are living hand to mouth. It is not just the shabby quality of the buildings—many are old mudbrick mansions hurriedly repurposed for selling things—it is the frantic energy with which pitchmen and women come at the pedestrians. I can see the enterprising, rebellious spirit at play, as theorists of informality would have it. I can also see the marginalization. But what I perceive more than anything is a tension in the air, a world caught between the strictures of bureaucracy and the abandon of transgressions that the logic of business cannot capture.

Other commercial venues are new but still shoddy constructions. They were supposed to replace street commerce ever since Mayor Alberto Andrade reorganized downtown in the 1990s. Instead, these enclosed markets are magnets for street vendors who, stationed in front of them, benefit from the foot traffic. Market vendors resent them, but they have other advantages. Market vendors are organized into associations and cooperatives, and they coalesce around elected leadership, a patron saint, and an active collective life. Informality and marginalization gloss over the different realities of the lone, self-employed peddler; the hired street or market salesperson; the market stand owner who may or may not own more vending stands elsewhere in the downtown area; the leader of an association; and, finally, the vendor who has access to the networks and financial, political, and material resources that associations make available.

Some kind of altar to a patron saint can usually be seen near a market's entrance. It took me longer than I would have liked to realize that immanent to this chaotic commercial world and the relationships it sustains is the vast pantheon of Catholic saints as well as Jesus Christ and the Virgin Mary in their various iterations. There are also the spirits

of the dead and the energies, powers, and acts through which they manifest their desires, reproaches, and generosity with the living. In such a social universe, the calculation between means and ends— whether with an eye to efficiency, profit, or growth—plays a part but within clear limits. Collective life, elevated above the quotidian, is nurtured through a busy yearly calendar of holidays, parties, anniversaries, patron saint festivities, and recreational activities. These are "detours of exuberance," to use Georges Bataille's phrase, that fulfill no ulterior function beyond a joyous overflow of life.

A culture of agonism compels donations for these events and participation in gift giving, mutual aid, and reciprocity of time and favors, which result in significant nonprofitable utilization of resources. There are also the recurrent losses connected to the unsociable extremes of negative reciprocity, from corruption and embezzlement to the continual police shutdowns and seizures of goods to the reality of destruction by fire, crowd trampling, and earthquakes. In their contravention of utility and accumulation as the ultimate goal, in their going beyond calculation and exceeding the imperative of productivity, vendors open up a space for the experience of sacredness. Their embrace of excess and loss, even sacrifice, demands a radical expansion of what we commonly understand by "the economy," so-called informal or otherwise.

I am never sure what I will find past the hustle and bustle I have to wade through to get to El Hueco's entrance. As I get closer, I wonder, Will the market be closed for an event? Will it be in the middle of a police raid or shut down because of a fire? Will it be undergoing construction for a building upgrade? Or will it, finally, be gone forever?

Today, when I enter El Hueco midmorning, a young man stands by the door with a microphone and loudspeaker. Music blares from the speaker while he pleads with vendors to keep their merchandise inside their stands. Displaying wares in the market's narrow corridors and common spaces is utterly prohibited, he says.

—It is dangerous, and God forbid the fiscal police might come by and close us down!

No one pays heed. I walk by a tall stack made up of reams of printing paper and other office supplies as I cross the courtyard inside the belowground market.

This is one ordinary day. But at El Hueco and Mesa Redonda, an ordinary day becomes extraordinary in a matter of seconds. The line between the two hardly exists. Every day contains, realized or potentially, all the risk, loss, and excess that so actively feed the imagination about this place, that attract or repulse them, and even both at once.

In what follows, I recount the events of one August 24th, the day the vendor cooperative of El Hueco celebrates the anniversary of its foundation. Both ordinary and extraordinary, that day crystallizes for me the kind of economic anthropology this and similar markets in downtown Lima call for, the attention it must give to transgression and exuberance, and the central place of storytelling in it.

❋

I

Morning

1

When I arrive early that day, a chunky chain of bright green and yellow balloons hangs around the entrance. The perky colors stand out against the gloomy drizzle and wet sidewalks. The storefronts on the rest of the block are still closed, and a handful of pedestrians, hunched against the cool, damp air walk by in a hurry, sidestepping the cracks on the cement where the drizzle pools. Only one of El Hueco's double swing doors is open. It gives onto the top of a ramp where a man in a suit wipes down the large frame of a painting of the Lord of Miracles.

I walk under the arch of balloons and pause in the threshold. The man hears or otherwise senses me because he turns around. He no more than glances at me, and without a word goes back to dusting the image of the market's patron saint.

Aside from more balloon decorations, everything looks the same as the day before: the signs welcoming shoppers, the screen blaring a music video clip, and the blue, translucent nylon tarp over the courtyard to stop the morning sprinkle from making a muddy mess. The tarp, which is tied with strings to the edges of the corrugated roofs, dims the little natural light that makes it into the sunken premises.

It is difficult to convey how flat the gray of Lima's sky is in August, the dead of winter. It lacks the luminosity or ominous feel overcast skies have in other places. It is uniformly dull and without the discernible swirl or swish of a cloud to add perspectival depth. And the fine Lima rain barely qualifies as precipitation. It is more like a saturation of the air so total that droplets build on surfaces and crevices, making sidewalks, ramps, and stairs grimy and slippery.

Even though Señor Arispe has invited me to attend the celebration, I walk down the ramp tentatively. He has asked me to call him Roberto, but it doesn't yet roll off the tongue. Addressing him as *usted*, at this point, sounds more like an affirmation of social distance. It can be of age or class. Roberto and I are close in age, but we come from faraway social universes. I am faintly aware that I fear male vendors will interpret my use of *tú*, along with my interest in their lives and businesses, as an opening for flirtation. This has happened. It comes with doing fieldwork in Lima if you are a woman. But I have known Roberto for eight years, and he is too serious and smart for that. I expect to see him today as well as the other vendors I know, but not Señora Emilia. She passed away recently. She was only in her early sixties. Her ailments, she once told me, were due to having worked too hard and suffered too much in her life.

The vendors have put together a program that goes from nine in the morning to an unspecified time at night. Halfway down the ramp, I see a string of shuttered vending stalls. It is a strange sight for a market open year-round and usually brimming with people, goods of eye-popping colors and textures, and music, TV chatter, and other busy noise. A long garland of fabric, also bright green and yellow, bobs around the oddly shaped perimeter of the property, clashing now with the drab, rusty metal doors. Lima journalists often scramble for the right words to depict this market, grasping for ever more degrading terms with which to capture its reprobate character and ill reputation.

"El Hueco is a motley commercial center housing about 1,400 vendors who cram inside a hollow," is how a reporter introduces his readers to the place. The rest of the article is dotted with words such as risk, threat, trinkets, minefield, dangerous, deficient, and overcrowded. Another reporter describes the market as a crater and a sinkhole. "The first impression when one takes a look inside," he writes about El Hueco, "is that it shouldn't be there."

But it is here. It has been here, wedged into one of downtown Lima's busiest intersections, for almost three decades, a painful thorn in the side of the city government.

2

In 1988, UNESCO designated the oldest blocks of Lima, founded by the Spaniards in 1535, as a "historic center" and World Heritage site. Inside the south end of the protected area, flouting its restrictive building code, is El Hueco. At the time of UNESCO's intervention, the property was an empty foundation pit that had been dug out four decades earlier for a state building that was never built. Visitors entering the market today are met eye level with a large banner welcoming its clientele:

CENTRO COMERCIAL "EL HUECO"
LE DA LA BIENVENIDA A TODA SU CLIENTELA

The vendors' ironic but total acceptance of the market's rather debasing moniker *hueco*—hole, pit, orifice, cavity, hollow—is never lost on me. There is an implicit hierarchy in the different kinds of vending arrangements one sees in Lima: *Paraditas* are street markets, the more precarious kind of commerce alongside itinerant vending. *Campos feriales* follow, with their prefabricated, one-story vending modules and open, corrugated roofs, and the wonky, brick-and-mortar multistory *galerías* are next. El Hueco, strictly speaking, is a campo ferial. Vendors would like it to be a *centro comercial*, a proper mall, and they try to conjure this desire into reality by calling themselves so. But over the years, I have come to realize that they want it to be a centro comercial and that they do not want it to be a centro comercial. Many of them fear moving too far away from the street level for higher floors and losing their competitive edge. It is not uncommon for such established businesses, those that achieve the dream of a respectable building, to feel the need to send salespeople back down to the streets. Folk wisdom is that it is there where one finds the best deals. Maybe it is because of its unlikely location belowground—which confers it a sketchy, netherworld feel—that in the pecking order of Lima's commercial world, El Hueco enjoys a privileged position of ignominy among the humble, semilegal campos feriales.

The market's property sits at the juncture of two major downtown thoroughfares. One is Abancay, a wide avenue that links, through an impossibly congested bridge over the Río Rímac, the historic center and the northern districts of the city. The other is Nicolás de Piérola, which crosses Abancay on its eighth block from the river. With its hundreds of microbuses inching along it, picking up and dropping off millions of travelers at all hours of the day, Abancay is a holdout of poorly regulated vending in the city center. There, it is still possible to see, in all its ebullience, the kind of entrepreneurship that inspired Hernando de Soto to argue forty years ago—just as the Shining Path carried out its bloody armed revolution in the central and southern Andes—that the most radical transformation of the social order in the history of Peru was actually taking place, in front of our very eyes, in the streets of Lima.

I first visited El Hueco one December morning in 2009 just as the stands were readied for Christmas and the sun broke through Lima's skies for the first time in months. It is difficult to convey the thrill of leaving behind Plaza Mayor, Lima's center of political power, and crossing Abancay to join the crowds on the other side, walking elbow to elbow along contrastingly crowded and unkempt streets past some shoe rubberizing stands, steamed corn carts, and vendors of peeled fruit until reaching the entrance to the market. The sweetly pungent smell of the discarded rinds rose from the ground and followed me inside. My eyes darted to the left and the right, drawn to the masterful displays of stuff, all sorts of stuff, exceeding the bounds of each stand. The thrill intensified knowing that I entered at my own peril. A sign by the door with the market's floor plan was dizzying rather than instructive. It seemed to validate the representations of El Hueco in the media as a dangerous place, impossible to escape during an earthquake or a fire. But the stands irresistibly lured me down the dim corridors with some sort of promise that, even today, I can't adequately explain.

When, after this initial visit, my friend Octavio learned that I was doing fieldwork at El Hueco, he grimaced in revulsion.

—That place is sordid!

I asked him to explain.

—The atmosphere . . . super ugly, lowly, marginal . . .

He hesitated, searching for a more precise term to convey El Hueco's illicit and clandestine aura. Apparently settled, he said:

—Lumpenesque. Yeah, that's the word I couldn't find.

Octavio worked as a sales rep for a pharmaceutical company and had recently tracked down some of his medical samples to El Hueco.

This is impermissible, an unforgivable lapse that put his job at risk. Before going inside, his boss, a woman, said to him, "Wait for me here." Minutes later, she came back out pale with fear. Vendors saw her approach, nicely dressed in her pantsuit, and somehow knew what she had come for. They rolled down the fronts of their stands and looked at her menacingly. She turned on her heels and ran back out without the medicines.

Lumpenesque. It wasn't the first time I heard someone refer to El Hueco that way. *Lumpen* is an abbreviation of *lumpenproletariat,* a term that in Marxism refers to people who do not quite qualify as part of the proletariat, the working class. In contrast to the proletariat, the lumpenproletariat lacks class consciousness of its oppression under capitalism and as a result is deemed to be politically opportunistic and unreliable for the revolutionary project. Members of the lumpen, furthermore, have no qualms transgressing the law. At El Hueco, vendors indeed live in a kind of legal limbo. The market has been known for decades as one of Lima's top wholesale distributors of pirated music and film content as well as knock-off and tampered goods. Yet vendors are well organized into a cooperative. To the frequent assaults in the media and the crises that follow every police intervention and confiscation of merchandise, vendors respond with strong collective action, banding together as a single corps. The market's spirit of collectivism is born of a shared history and struggle. But if this collectivism is always palpable, so are the obvious undercurrents of self-interest and *desconfianza,* or distrust. The cooperative is at once obstinately horizontal in its structure and irredeemably individualistic and defiant. This is what makes the market what it is, what has allowed it to survive for decades, but also what limits its growth and jeopardizes its consolidation into a centro comercial.

3

The explosions of green and yellow—the market's adopted colors— extend deep into the maze of corridors. There are also inflatable beer and champagne bottles. "¡FELIZ ANIVERSARIO!" read banners of blowup bubble letters. Each corridor showcases plumper wreaths, bows, and balloon chains than the other. I hear that there will be a prize for the best, most dazzling decoration.

Two young men in working overalls join the man in a suit readying the Lord of Miracles for his short procession down to the courtyard inside the hole. One helps with the wiping, and the other sprinkles sawdust on the wet cement surface for grip. Down below, people set up an altar table and chairs for an opening mass. Above their heads, through the sheer blue fabric tied to the roofs, the top stories of a building across the avenue loom. It is the tower whose twin replica, planned for the hole inside which I am now standing, never went up. Originally home to the Ministry of Education, today the tower houses Lima's Superior Courts. At eighty-six meters and twenty-two stories high, it was, at the time of its inauguration in 1956, the tallest building in Lima and an icon of the modernist spirit that had gripped the city. By 1958 the twin tower's construction had already been called off and its foundation pit left to languish.

The man in a suit clinks a bell three times. On cue, eight men, four positioned on each side of the effigy, lift the portable platform—called *anda*, from *andar*, to walk—onto their shoulders. Shuffling their feet under it, the Lord of Miracles slowly walks down the ramp and settles next to the altar.

I spot Señor Arispe—Roberto. He is helping place the chairs in rows. A woman slips white ruffled covers over the front row chairs. It seems to be for the VIPs. Roberto sees me and comes over. He wants me to meet the new cooperative president, a tall, lanky man several years older than him. Roberto is wearing his signature aviator jacket and baseball cap over his balding head. The new president sports a sleek, navy blue suit. The president and I shake hands and exchange courtesies.

—Mucho gusto.

—Manuel Condori, para servirle.

Another man of surname Sánchez—I don't catch his first name—stands by Señor Condori. He is another member of the current administration. Señor Sánchez speaks with a syrupy voice, eyeing me up and down.

—Who's your friend?

The man teases Roberto at my expense. As I said, it comes with the territory. Roberto ignores him. He taps Señor Condori in the arm and takes off.

—Con permiso.

The sleazy guy gets the message and beats the retreat behind Roberto. I try to fill in the awkward silence.

—It's an impressive anda.

But from where we are, near the base of the ramp, the Lord does look stunning in his large wooden platform. He is surrounded by an ornate, silver-and-gold frame, four silver angels, and four silver vases with bright yellow flowers and green spear leaves. More tall vases with flowers are placed on the ground at his feet and before the altar. I fumble some more for a conversation starter.

—It's clear people here care about him.

Señora Emilia, a cooperative founding member and seller of towels, linens, and socks, once told me that, back in the late 1990s, when the vendors first tried to level the ground inside the hole to prime it as a market, their efforts failed. The excavators brought in to do the work broke down on contact with the soil. The monetary contributions for the costly endeavor were lost, stolen, or wasted. Conflict reigned. The reason was that in the 1880s the property had been expropriated from the Carmelite Convent of Santa Teresa and the Hospice of Santa Rosa de Candamo, and the evicted nuns had placed a curse on it so that any attempt to build there would be fruitless. That was the source of all their problems. Señora Emilia said that the lot had to be exorcised and a supreme sovereign, the Lord of Miracles, put in charge and regularly feasted for the whole thing to work.

Señor Condori agrees.

—We do care.

The Lord is the reason for everything. He is the reason Condori himself has had success. His son is almost done with his engineering degree, and his daughter is in medical school. He is proud, he says, but it has not been easy.

—Do you know where I began?

He doesn't wait for an answer to tell me that it feels like yesterday when he peddled on Jirón de la Unión, a crowded commercial offshoot of Lima's main plaza. His wife owned a sewing machine. She made jogging pants, and he sold them in the street. All day sewing, all day selling. No rest. Arduous times. Lots of struggle. But it was worth it. He is grateful to him, he says, pointing across the courtyard to the altar, where the Lord of Miracles sits still and self-possessed as tears well up in Señor Condori's eyes.

A young priest decked in a hooded alb taps a microphone to test it. A strident noise reverberates inside the market. Condori invites me to sit down. The mass is about to begin.

I sit on the fourth row, behind a woman with flaming red hair and a coat with faux fur-trim collar. She turns around to chat. She has things to say. Her name is Olvido, which means forgetfulness or oblivion in Spanish, and she is a vending-stand owner's sister. She remarks on the span of time the cooperative has existed.

—Thirty-four years! And to think that this place was going to be a psychiatric hospital.

I nod even though I don't really know what she is talking about. The hospice of Santa Rosa de Candamo used to be next to Santa Teresa, but a psychiatric hospital? I have never heard such a thing. But I am not exactly surprised. A weird and intriguing mix of facts, oral histories, storytelling, lore, conspiracy narratives, and urban tall tales infuses the public discourse about El Hueco.

—Look how empty it is. They don't know what they're doing.

Olvido points to the rows behind me. Her righteous observation betrays not so much concern as a tinge of satisfaction in the fact that, so close to the planned starting time, less than a third of the chairs are occupied. Is she voicing her sister's discontent? But who are *they*? I ask Olvido why she thinks more people aren't there.

—It's because of—she pauses for emphasis and then punctuates each syllable—*di-fe-ren-cias* with the president.

The word is loaded with a meaning that I have spent a long time trying to grasp.

Ever since the cooperative, officially the Cooperativa de Servicios Especiales Mercado Central Limitada (COOPSE), was created in 1983, and then since it moved into the corner hole, the vendors have upheld the *cooperativismo* ideals of egalitarianism, solidarity, and mutual aid and have simultaneously behaved like rivals or enemies, hurling endless accusations of embezzlement, kickbacks, solicitation, or just plain corruption at one another. An unspoken question quietly hovers over my exchange with Olvido: How can egalitarianism and reciprocity coexist with such levels of conflict and suspicion? In fact this question has hovered over all my exchanges with vendors over the years, and it lingers as I write these lines.

4

Gloria Cranmer Webster, a member of the Kwakwaka'wakw First Nation of the Pacific Northwest, writes that "potlatch means 'to give.'"
Potlatch in that region is a communal feast held during the cold winter
months, in which the hosts consume to the end accumulated resources
in honor of their guests. While partaking with ancestors and passing on
hereditary rights, including to bare certain names and own songs, are
central to the ritual profligacy of potlatches, the circulation of property
in the form of gifts and the destruction of valuables by fire were, at least
until the turn of the twentieth century, also important components at
these winter ceremonials.

Potlatches depended on a spring and summer, and often longer,
of labor amassing goods. Cranmer Webster's elders said that prepa-
rations for one could take years. The goods included the products of
fishing, hunting, gathering, weaving cedar-bark blankets, collecting fish
oil, carving wood objects, and sheering and hammering copper breast
plates—all highly prized valuables to be regaled on guests. Inside a
chief's big house, with a great fire burning in the middle, hundreds of

guests and their hosts would gather for days and even weeks to dance, sing, and give speeches, as the guests were lavished with presents and food, and the hosts further displayed their generosity by pouring great quantities of fish oil and sometimes wood-carved canoes into the fire, which grew so big that it threatened to burn the house down. The U'Mista Cultural Society of the Kwakwa̱ka̱'wakw explains that "many people believe that a rich and powerful person is someone who has a lot. . . . For [us], the wealthiest people are those who not only accumulate the most stuff, but also give it all away in a potlatch, as a sign of their ability to do so."

In a detailed account of going on the annual "grease trail" with her family to collect eulachon oil, Cranmer Webster describes the arduous labor of catching and extracting the oil of the tiny but fat-rich fish. An important food and item for trade with villages in the interior, eulachon oil has always also featured prominently in potlatches. "Among our people," Cranmer Webster writes, "a potlatch at which large quantities of grease are given away is unique." She goes on:

> Part of the ceremony requires the host family to "feed" the central fire in the big house by pouring grease on it, indicating that the family is so wealthy that it can afford to squander such a precious commodity in such an extravagant fashion. While the fire is being fed, members of the host's family sing feast songs that can only be described as arrogant and full of pride. For example, my father's feast song refers to a column of smoke rising that is so huge that it can be seen all over the world. This is the smoke from the fire of the chief, who uses the canoes of lesser chiefs as kindling.

In the 1920s, Marcel Mauss rendered potlatch as "to consume," like the roaring, big-house fire consumes the oil. Mauss relied on Franz Boas's and George Hunt's field reports about the Kwakwa̱ka̱'wakw world, where, incidentally, an Indigenous word for the feasts did not exist. The term originated in the trading jargon of the Chinook and grew to become a catchall for all winter ceremonials marked by excessive giving through its use in letters and reports by white settlers and officials of the nascent Canadian nation, who in 1885 banned the practice. For those officials, the feasts violated what was reasonable from an economic point of view. The practice of accumulating property solely for the purpose of giving it away, sometimes to the point of poverty, threatened the bourgeois values and capitalist ideals behind their civilizing mission.

Through Mauss, the feasts of the Kwakwa̱ka̱'wakw became the classic example of potlatch in the anthropological literature, and he relied on the term to conceptually affirm an attitude of openhanded generosity as "a general potentiality among all human groups," in Holly High's words. Soon, potlatch became a stand-in for forms of giving away or consuming resources for others without a guarantee that they would be reciprocated or produce returns of any kind. This is an aberration from the perspective of political economy, which, as Karl Polanyi explained in the 1940s, assumes a human predisposition toward self-interest and achieving maximum gains. I am attracted to El Hueco precisely because it evokes a problem that has haunted anthropology for a long time. It is the problem of potlatch, of what to make of a people's inclination to collectively and without profit spend the surplus of their production, redistribute it, or accept its periodic destruction and loss.

At El Hueco, profits and donations fund a rich yearly calendar of events to mark—with gifts, food, drink, speeches, music, and dance—holidays such as Labor Day, Mother's Day, Father's Day, Women's Day, and Pledge of Allegiance Day in addition to the anniversary of their cooperative, camaraderie trips to the countryside, thermal bath retreats, and lengthy soccer championships. It also funds educational and mutual aid programs for vendors. The white settlers and officials in Canada deemed the feasts they came to call potlatch irrational and wasteful. They believed they kept First Nations peoples, as U'Mista puts it, "from becoming civilized." For who gives away their amassed wealth without return, stunting their own progress? Who lets their possessions burn up and willingly becomes vulnerable to the destructive, sacrificial capacities of fire?

This is also how Lima officials and the media perceive El Hueco for the way vendors upend the logic of maximizing utility in favor of a use of surpluses not as a means to the end of economic growth but as an end in itself. Their commitment to redistribution and an intense collective life points to an economy that is "completely absorbed by the intensely vivid experiences which offer superabundant noneconomic motivation." It directs us to focus, in other words, not so much on processes of production and exchange but on forms of consumption, on the ways vendors care to spend their surpluses. Bataille explains that "a society always produces more than is necessary for its survival; it has a surplus at its disposal. . . . It is precisely the use it makes of this surplus that determines it." I think of this dictum in relation to El Hueco and Mesa Redonda all the time and to vendors' desire for autonomy, immoderate proclivities, and willingness to risk the loss of everything, every day, to fires or police confiscations in order to live and work the way they want.

There are many examples in Euro-American history and society of uses of great surpluses of wealth that, from the perspective of classical economics, are less than sensible: from the maintenance of sovereigns and a royalty class, with their splendid palaces and estates, to Christianity's cathedrals, the carnivals of yesteryear, and the carnivals and festivals of today, such as Mardi Gras and Burning Man, to mention only a few. Bataille and the literature that builds on his work discuss many more. So why don't we have a common word in our vocabulary for forms of spending surplus wealth that place the accent on loss, on the withdrawal of that wealth from circulation? Potlatch filled a conceptual void that Bataille must have felt when he decided to reserve the French *dépense* for it. Translated as "expenditure," dépense, in Bataille's lexicon, refers to the profitless utilization of resources and the excesses occasioned by such forms of consumption.

The richness of life enabled by potlatch-like immoderation casts light on the inadequacy of political economy to effectively grasp the range of a society's material life processes without pathologizing, condemning, or demeaning it. It calls into question the deep-seated idea that social worlds like El Hueco and Mesa Redonda suffer from a state of underdevelopment and urban malaise or exist as the result of marginalization. The vendors' techniques of livelihood rather derail political economy's teleology of progress and enfranchisement and undo the boundaries between the supposedly discrete and transcendent spheres of politics, religion, ethics, and especially economics in its reductive, business-like definition.

5

Roberto and I met the last time he was president of the cooperative. It was 2010. One afternoon, I visited him up in his office, a small room with a lone window looking out on the market's rooftop, a patchwork of

rusty corrugated tin slats. It faced the area where his own stand, a printing and engraving business, gives onto Abancay. He and I stood there
as Roberto shared his opinion of El Hueco's most serious problem:

—The low level of the people—he said.

I did a double take before writing it down, reluctantly, in my
notebook.

—People here have little education. El Hueco is a jumble of cul-
tures: former teachers, retirees, policemen, taxi drivers, middle class,
upper class, traders at heart, and former street vendors. It's hard to find
points of agreement with so many ways of thinking.

Now including himself in his critical appraisal of vendors, he said:

—We don't know about investing toward the future. We don't see
the future, only the present.

As president of the cooperative, Roberto supported the construction of a mall-type building. He said that because there is ignorance
among vendors, the Education Committee under his administration
had developed a plan to "re-educate" them so they could see the benefits
of such expansion. The committee hired professionals at Universidad
Católica—a major expense for the cooperative, one can assume—to
teach them classes on business planning, project administration, and
finance. But vendors are not interested in investing in the future. They
are spendthrifts.

—They say, "Ah! I don't mind spending all my week's earnings!"

Roberto parroted vendors' foolhardy attitude and then concluded:

—They spend without thinking about risk. They live in the moment. There is no prevention.

I didn't know what to make of Roberto's derisive comments, especially since I knew he himself belonged to the lowest rung on his list:
vendors who started selling in the streets. I took note of every term of
(self-)contempt as the depth of the rifts among cooperative members
became clearer.

Roberto grumbled that vendors had approved his building initiative only to reject it later because of rumors of corruption. Suddenly,
the problem behind the frustrated construction project was no longer
ignorance. It was no longer vendors' irrational spending habits or in-
ability to invest in the future. Now it was more straightforwardly their
complicated, worn-out relationships, dominated as they were by feelings of resentment and distrust.

A few days later, leafing through a copy of El Hueco's yearly newsletter, I would see that charges of corruption were flying in every direction. In it, the head of the Education Committee claims that Roberto had unduly influenced the election of members in his committee while Roberto retorts that the previous administrative council—in which the head of the Education Committee had served—had embezzled money. All this just as the president of an ad hoc Building Committee casts doubts on Roberto's motivations for revoking its members on suspicion of kickbacks and promises to fight the accusations.

Out of the blue, Roberto opened the door and showed me out.

—Let's go down. I'll introduce you to someone.

I followed right behind.

Señora Emilia sat on a stool in front of her stand. The stand was at the crossroads of two main corridors that roughly divide El Hueco into four sections. It was dark and cramped that deep inside the hole. Only a few faint rays of natural light and a chilly draft slipped in through the gaps in the ridged ceilings. The stands are about two by two meters, and the walls of Señora Emilia's were draped with her merchandise: socks in plastic wrappers, terrycloth bathrobes, and towels with prints of animals, soccer team logos, curvaceous women, and superheroes. I spotted one with two tiger cubs, and my heart was instantly set on it for my toddler son. On a countertop were more towels, neatly folded and sorted into piles. She pulled a spare stool out from under the countertop for me to join her.

Señora Emilia's stories poured out of her. She spoke about the cooperative's early days, rising occasionally to refold a towel or rearrange a pile.

—I began on the fifth block of Jirón Huallaga—she said.

Jirón Huallaga is one of the streets where vendors had settled around Mercado Central. This was the early 1980s. In 1983 a young city council member named Luis Castañeda Lossio, who would later go on to serve three terms as mayor of Lima, persuaded Señora Emilia and a few dozen other vendors to organize into a cooperative. The idea was to find strength in numbers to fight off the government's eviction threats. As a founding member, Señora Emilia knew the ins and outs of the cooperative like no other, having over the years served in its administration in several capacities. She explained that the cooperative is structured to curb ownership and control by limiting members to only one share.

—With regards to property there is a single right. No one can own more than one stand. It is one stand, one vote.

I was impressed by the built-in horizontality and the deliberate restrictions on individual economic and political power.

The cooperative, she went on to say, is run by administrative council and one hundred delegates elected by thirds every year by majority vote. As a current delegate herself, she said her relationship with vendors was one of mutual cooperation.

—Between members and delegates, it is a reciprocity. We are a communal agreement.

This agreement, however, is often brittle and not quite binding, Señora Emilia explained. A delegate's main duty is to share information, to orient and persuade, and to assuage concerns. It is also to represent, but cooperative members and delegates change their minds on issues all the time and freely withdraw their support. Even after a binding vote at general assembly, cliques and factions form, Señora Emilia said. Divisiveness and reservations arise that lead to de facto overturned decisions and truncated projects, like the construction of their commercial center, which has been voted on favorably a few times but remains in limbo. Señora Emilia made it clear to me that she had been among those wishing to defer construction. She didn't want to pay rent elsewhere to keep her businesses going while they built.

As I walked back to Roberto's office, I glanced at a billboard in the courtyard with a mockup of the projected building, a modern, slick, glass-enveloped structure—an anti-Hueco, if you will—with a date of June 2010 to break ground. That date had just come and gone. Rusty and ramshackle, El Hueco kept on going impassively, at once ghostly and real, silently flaunting its presence inside the historic center and its defiance toward the law.

Since the year we met, Roberto has stayed away from elected office. He prefers working behind the scenes, motivated in equal parts by a can-do attitude and a fatalistic but stoic frustration. Sometimes the latter prevails. Once, on another visit, he conceded that there is nothing in Lima's commercial regulations that could protect El Hueco from definitive closure. The market is, in every respect—at the level of zoning, the building code, and civil defense—in violation of the law. The reason they remain open, he said, is political. But how long can that last?

Vendors have capitalized on the denigratory reference to their market as a hueco, turning their renown for astuteness, knavery, and lax standards—the basis of their supposed rock-bottom prices—into a huge point of attraction. But if this is the market's strength, it is also its main weakness. To succeed not in spite but because of its infamy and insecure status and to depend on the favoritisms of a particular political moment is a risky, double-edged tactic that could easily backfire.

—After all—Roberto said to me that day—we are, well, a hole!

6

The mass starts. About half of the chairs are now occupied. The men on the VIP seats wear suits and the women skirts and formal blazers. They are all well past their middle age years and are probably members of the market's founding generation: the cooperative's elders. Despite the Sunday best outfits, they look haggard. They have the weary, weathered look of people after a lifetime of labor outdoors, battling the elements.

The priest grabs his guitar and leads the attendants in song. An old violin player joins him by the altar. A Quechua tune follows one in Spanish. Many in the seats sing along and clap animatedly. They seem moved to be singing in Quechua, maybe the language they first spoke as children, which I have not heard used at El Hueco before. In his homily, the priest volunteers that he is *huancavelicano*, conveying that he also hails from the Andes and eliciting cheers. He then launches into a sermon on the importance of living in peace, in harmony, no matter where anyone is from, no matter "our differences"—again, that barefaced euphemism. He doesn't give specifics. The need to live harmoniously is, from then on, the main theme in his and the rest of the day's speeches:

—We must not fight, not offend, but get along.

The statement vaguely points to the long-standing stalemate the vendors find themselves in. Only the insistent cadence of these

words—peace, harmony, differences—from speaker to speaker gives
a hint of how high the stakes are and how intractable the conflict. If
the backdrop of this elaborate anniversary event—full of festoons and
promising good food, drink, and live dance music—is still a rickety,
prefabricated structure, the reality is that the structure sits on a more
than nine thousand square meter millionaire property, and many vendors are ready to invest eighty million dollars more in a multistory
upgrade. But vendors are unable to reconcile their individual and their
collective needs and interests, and thus no agreement ever holds on
how to move forward.

By the time of communion, all the chairs are taken, and more people
stand on the sides. Many elders no longer work at their stands. They
rent them out or hire salespeople to do the long shifts with nothing
but a few breaks to eat their meals without leaving their posts. Those in
the standing crowd seem to be curious onlookers more than partakers,
probably some of the hundreds of renters and sales employees, the
lesser beneficiaries of the prosperity of beleaguered El Hueco.

None of the old vendors, as my chat with Señor Condori attests,
have to be reminded of the hardship in getting to where they are now.
But that is exactly what happens once the mass ends. The man who

had earlier dusted off the Lord's image stands on a podium and plays the MC. He begins by reading the entire Foundation Act of the vendor cooperative, in which only eighty-three vendors, the original members, are signatories. It is as if the elders in fact need reminding of the precarity of life back then, the repression, the terrible odds that they would ever grow out of the survival economy that had put them, in the first place, on the streets. The MC reads into the microphone:

—General Assembly for the constitution of the Cooperativa de Servicios Especiales Mercado Central Limitada in the city of Lima on the 24th day of the month of August of 1983 . . .

His solemn voice, amplified, bounces off the enclosure walls.

—In order to give an account of the work carried out by the members of the organizing committee to establish the cooperative that the street vendors of Mercado Central and adjacencies planned to alleviate the problems they have in the face of the threat of eviction from the streets they occupy to sell their products and looking for a safe place to be able to build an appropriate locale that will be the cooperative market . . .

The cooperative was thus created and inscribed in the public registers, but the vendors continued to work out of their makeshift street posts around Mercado Central for over a decade, a period spanning at least three city administrations. Then, in 1996, the perennial threat of eviction of street vendors and peddlers intensified when Mayor Andrade, a native of the downtown neighborhood of Barrios Altos, took office. Downtown Lima had become the realization of an old and widespread fear, one deeply shared by Andrade, of a city besieged by Indigenous people and peasants from the highlands. Andrade thus spearheaded the most aggressive makeover of the city center in half a century, beginning precisely with the streets around Mercado Central.

7

It was the predawn hours of a mid-May morning in 1997. A few blocks south of Lima's Plaza Mayor, around five thousand vendors were entrenched in the streets. They had partitioned the sidewalks and pavement around Mercado Central and built a tight belt of wobbly but permanent stands that choked the market building out of any business. Andrade, Lima's new mayor, had welcomed the neoliberal policies of President Alberto Fujimori's undemocratic regime (1990–2000) and understood his own undertaking to beautify and reorder Lima to be aligned with those policies. This included the expulsion of vendors from their posts in every downtown street and plaza.

That early morning, the municipal police moved in to block the vendors from reaching their posts on Jirón Huallaga only to be attacked with "gangster rage," as a weekly news magazine put it, by a mob that was two thousand strong and that vastly outnumbered the unarmed municipal force. Molotov cocktails rained down on the astonished sentries, forcing them to retreat, burned and bloody.

Andrade's downtown cleanup campaign came in the wake of a long period of runaway inflation, car bomb attacks by the Shining Path, and antiterrorist measures that had left the center of Lima in very bad shape. Starting in the mid-1980s, traffic into downtown had slowed to a trickle because of barricaded streets around state offices, banks, and media companies, which were favorite targets of the bombs. Much of the center looked like a war zone—eerily quiet, dotted with tanks and armed soldiers, its windowpanes crisscrossed with duct tape to prevent the glass from shattering, and left to decline and accumulate garbage. Like other streets and plazas west and south of Plaza Mayor, the blocks around Mercado Central across Abancay were equally neglected, but they bustled with the energy and ingenuity of a street economy that, amid the financial and political crisis, had flourished after four decades of steady migration to the city. The small middle-class contingent that still lived in the center moved out, and the bars, restaurants, and businesses catering to them closed down. Andrade thus cast his urban renewal initiative as the "recuperation" of the city center—recuperation, all at once, from terrorist destruction, government neglect, bourgeois oblivion, and migrant invasion.

A few hours after the failed eviction attempt, it was business as usual on Jirón Huallaga. The vending posts reopened to sell electronics, clothes, shoes, produce, and recycled and stolen goods to the tens of thousands of shoppers who walked through the street market each day. Photographs of it published in those years—often taken from a bird's eye view to emphasize its crowdedness and squalor—were meant to appall, to provoke outrage. And they did appall, but they also sparked the imagination.

The photographs show a sea of crude rooftops: scraps of metal, wood, tarps, and cardboard held down with stones and bricks. They bring to mind the imagery Friedrich Engels conjured as he walked the slums of early industrial Manchester and denounced, "Refuse, offal, and sickening filth!" In the poverty and dirt, Engels saw signs of promiscuity and crime, betraying, in his indignation, his bourgeois sensibility and moralism. In these pictures of Jirón Huallaga, one is meant to also see signs of *mal vivir*. One is meant to see the dens of lowlifes the media said the market harbored: burglars, purse snatchers, glue sniffers, and vagabonds—the riff raff of downtown equal to the market's morass. Was this true? Who knows. The street market offended; that is clear from the photographs. It is also clear that it attracted customers in droves. More than the central market proper.

In the weeks that followed, the national police moved in to assist in the removal of vendors. Once the vending posts were bulldozed, the parasitic dimension of the street market manifested in hundreds of electric connections that pilfered power from public cabling. It was obvious this was how vendors kept the market lit at night, but it was still shocking to see the pirate hookups in the light of day. The streets had then to be cleared of rats and tons of garbage. As with Engels's moralism, the outsize attention media outlets put on the vermin and waste, rather than on the elimination of thousands of livelihoods, betrayed racism and class prejudice; it betrayed the fact that the street markets were perceived as *cholo* spaces. In the 1980s and 1990s, the word cholo derived its virulence from its link to dirt and disorder, qualities imputed to the bodies and spaces of Andean immigrants, who for many had polluted and deformed Lima's life and culture from within. Thus, grievances about how Lima had been clean in the past and now was dirty were not actually based on a temporal reality but on perceptions of social difference. They grew out of a nostalgia for an illusory time and space based on a prior physical distance that threatened to completely disappear.

After the eviction from the streets of Mercado Central, a third of vendors moved to Avenida Argentina on the center's west end to create a commercial emporium of poorly regulated stands known as Las Malvinas. Hope was high that they would settle there and go legit, but news reports said that the area had soon turned into a *cachina*, a hub for the resale of stolen cell phones, computers, and digital cameras at crazy low prices. Another third of the evicted vendors moved north of the center. Emotions ran high, rivalries intensified. Some said their leader

stole the funds vendors had collected for the relocation. Others said it was a rival vying for her position who falsely accused her in order to oust her. The leader was eventually murdered.

The last group of vendors didn't go very far from Mercado Central. They moved into the hole of Abancay. In 1989, at the height of the armed conflict with the Shining Path and one of the worst economic crises Peruvians had ever experienced, President Alan García (1985–1990) ordered the Sociedad de Beneficencia de Lima, the city's oldest public charity agency, which owned the cursed foundation pit, to sell it to COOPSE. It was a brazen populist move at a time of near societal collapse, made acceptable by the fact that downtown Lima's real estate values were at an all-time low. In 1998, when the government allowed the displaced vendors to move into the hole after some minimal infrastructure work, it was under the condition that it be a temporary solution, only until they could build something sturdy.

This is how the market of El Hueco was born.

8

A wedge of El Hueco's property is on street level. There, the cooperative owns a number of stands that it rents out to vendors, and it runs two sets of for-pay bathrooms, each with a turnstile that lets users in for fifty cents of a sol, the Peruvian currency. For this amount they receive a wad of toilet paper and access to basic but clean facilities, which are scarce downtown. The stand rentals and bathrooms are an important source of revenue for the cooperative. So is a nearby food court area, also on street level and with a balcony that overlooks the courtyard inside. On regular days concession stands prepare hot meals and fruit juices and cater to vendors, who eat in their stands, sometimes while keeping an eye on a child playing or napping on the floor. This aspect of El Hueco and other downtown Lima markets drive city functionaries to despair: kids rolling on the ground, food prepared under who knows what sanitation standards, and vendors eating while working.

I take the stairs up to the food court area hoping to get a hot tea to fight the bone-chilling humidity, but all the kitchens are busy making huge pots of *cabrito a la norteña*, goat stew with rice and boiled yuca, lunch for the thousand or so people I estimate are in attendance now. Down below, the reading of the Act goes on. It is a commemoration of the vendors' plight as well as a retelling of the market's origin story. The MC finishes by reading all eighty-three names of the founders. Those who are present get up from their VIP seats and stand in line. They will take turns addressing the audience. A small crowd forms around me to watch from the balcony, and we are slowly engulfed in the garlicky smell of cooking rice.

As the elders speak, I notice other scenes of action. To my right is a tower with dozens of crates of one-liter beer bottles. To my left men lay thick cables for two giant speakers and several electronic instruments that are scattered on the floor. The large quantities of beer and live band equipment are a hint of where the day is headed. The scenes bring me right back to the office of César Miranda, head of the Formalization Division at the municipal government until 2011.

Miranda led perhaps the most serious effort to legalize—in official parlance, to formalize or regularize—El Hueco and the hundreds of galerías and campos feriales in Mesa Redonda. He believed that a modicum of control and supervision over these troublemaker markets could be gained by making them obtain an operating license. He would at least have them on the books and could require periodic inspections. Miranda had a degree in business administration, but—tall, gangly, and always in slacks and rolled-up sleeves—his biggest asset was his approachable manner. Many vendors trusted him. He and his boss in

the office of Commercial Development lobbied to allow campos feriales in the historic center, where they are prohibited, to be eligible for
licenses if they met basic civil-defense safety criteria.

Ordinance 1209 passed as a result, a city law overriding the requirement of a brick-and-mortar building to qualify for a license. Lima's
urban planners, for whom eyesores like El Hueco should simply be removed from downtown, were indignant. With that major hurdle out of
the way, Miranda got to work. He gave out dozens of licenses to galerías
and campos feriales that could reach the much lower bar of Ordinance
1209. Miranda's office was soon after shut down, however, when Susana
Villarán, the only leftist mayor Lima has had since the early 1980s, took
office after Castañeda Lossio's second term.

One day, I visited Miranda in his office. He was presiding over a
meeting with his team to plan a field outing to El Hueco and Mesa
Redonda when a visitor was announced. It was Hilda Quezada, a stand
owner at Galería Adonis on Jirón Azángaro. Señora Quezada had vol-
unteered to rally the other owners and process her galería's license. She
wanted to inform Miranda of her progress.

—Galería Adonis, everything having to do with beauty—she said
for my benefit—is made up of salons and cosmetic stores.

The salons needed an abundant supply of water and electricity, but
they were not all outfitted with sinks and meters. Señora Quezada
spoke of the difficulty of exacting payment to cover the common
charges for these utilities. Imagine having to exact payment for things
like licenses, which, compared to running water and power, salon
owners deem superfluous. They had all agreed to obtain the license,
but when she approached them to collect the fee, they refused to pay.
Only when she adopted an extreme measure and ordered the security
guards to shut down the galería during peak hours did she see some
money trickle in.

Business owners do not like paying dues, Señora Quezada said.

—It's understandable when the person is just starting, but later . . .

Her statement suggested what is obvious to anyone walking in the
vicinity of Abancay: that most businesses are anything but hurting for
revenues.

—However—Señora Quezada went on—there is never a problem
collecting for our patron saint feast and anniversary party.

The next day, Miranda fleshed out the point.

—These vendors have money. You go to their parties, and you don't believe your eyes. They celebrate their anniversaries, go all out for their patron saints. They are great devotees, and what they donate!

He rummaged through a desk drawer looking for an old invitation to show me.

—They list the donations on them: thirty cases of beer . . . fifty of this . . . fifty of that . . .

Miranda said that, for their parties, vendors at Las Malvinas on Avenida Argentina block off the road, and, despite their real or imagined poverty, they have an all-out extravaganza. The Backus Corporation, the largest producer and distributor of beer in Peru, donates the assemblage and use of a stage—an incentive, it can be assumed, for all the beer party attendees will consume. This is, Miranda said, if the vendors do not opt for renting a more expensive indoor venue for the occasion. These are the same vendors who, time and again and often with a straight face, will tell city officials like Miranda that they do not have money to pay or make the improvements needed for a license.

Miranda looked genuinely confused. The economy of places like El Hueco appear to abide by two incompatible sets of values—Larissa Lomnitz calls them rival ideologies—whereby a shrewd understanding of market rationality and a strong work ethic coexist with ideas and behaviors inimical to that rationality and ethic. The daily exigencies of for-profit business do not detract from vendors' high tolerance for uncertainty and risk of closure or confiscation, or from their proclivity to spend lavishly for moments of collective joy and celebration. These are for the enjoyment of vendors and patron saints and have no obvious promotional ends. As I look out to the beer and to the band instruments, I, like Miranda, strain to make sense of it.

I think of piracy. Side by side with the Superior Courts' modernist tower, El Hueco, as a hub of piracy, is like the tower's negation. The blue tarp above the courtyard reminds me of Dorota Biczel's description of a structure built in the 1980s by Los Bestias. Like El Hueco, the structure had a thin fabric tied to the top that made it look like the sail of a pirate ship. Los Bestias was a Lima collective of architecture students whose works rejected their discipline's formal ideals because of their elitism in a city whose growth was driven largely by pirate-urbanization tactics. Pirate urbanization refers to the illicit takeover of city spaces that give way to sprawling shanties built with improvised materials and connections to services, as was then happening in Lima and many cities in the global south. AbdouMaliq Simone understands this kind of urban piracy more expansively to include the remaking of urban life through the "act of taking things out of their normal or legitimate framework of circulation and use" to generate disorientation as a way of creating opportunities for advancement in the city. Disorientation is exactly what markets like El Hueco and Mesa Redonda incite with their in-your-face visibility and simultaneous inscrutability.

Piracy, as a historical concept, has a political and even utopian dimension. It has been imagined as the basis for proto-Enlightenment experiments in egalitarianism and horizontal forms of government. Seventeenth-century pirate communities have also been imagined, informed by Bataille's expenditure and potlatch in much the same way I imagine El Hueco and Mesa Redonda today: as intentional communities that are collectivist, festive, wasteful, autonomous, and, yes, also insurrectionary and dedicated to "grim business."

9

But we do have a word. Or rather, a few of them: squanderer, spendthrift, profligate, wastrel, extravagant. They are all negative descriptors that convey the sense that to accumulate wealth and spend it immoderately or profitlessly is ignoble or at least questionable behavior. But this is not always perceived as such. Some expenditures are deemed noble, high minded, and worthy of respect.

Every year, the *Chronicle of Philanthropy* announces its list of the fifty top philanthropists. The billionaires are listed in descending order according to the size of their gifts. In 2024, Bill Gates and Warren Buffett ranked number one and number two, respectively, with billions of dollars given away. Buffet, for his part, is well known for having committed to divest from all his wealth during his lifetime or at death. If expenditures like these are regarded as magnanimity, it is only partly because they are directed toward laudable causes; they are regarded as magnanimity also because, as Bataille notes, they stem from and are reinforcing of a power the giver already possesses, the "power to lose." When exercised, this power accrues more power and honor for those who freely dispose of their wealth in this way. That a generous gesture elicits such an unprompted return is grounds for a utilitarian reading of gift giving and sacrifice as a mutually useful exchange in which givers and receivers—whether humans, gods, spirits, the earth, or the cosmos as a whole—gain something, be it wealth, power, status, good fortune, renown, equality, stability, or peace.

Bataille wrestled with this paradox: In the giving of a gift or the making of a sacrifice, expenditures generate a feeling of indebtedness and trigger a return in the form of an equivalent or something else of value. If a gift, as ordinary definitions have it, is something given gratuitously and for nothing, why is there the boomerang effect of a countergift, even if just in the form of recognition, like on the list of philanthropists? Mauss also understood this to be a contradiction, but for him the boomerang effect was essential to a gift's function. He explained that in gift giving and in sacrifice, selflessness and abandon intermingle, as they must, with self-interest and calculation, for their ultimate objective is to make and maintain relationships. What is a "society" if not these cycles and networks of reciprocal giving and receiving? He thus advises moderation, avoiding the harmful, antisocial extremes of

bourgeois individualism and too little giving, on the one hand, and of nonreciprocal overgenerosity, on the other.

Bataille, in contrast to Mauss, sought a way out of this contradiction. He believed our difficulties in unraveling it are rooted in a compulsory need to assign a function or attribute an ulterior motive to everything we do. The expectation, he argued, is that every action we undertake, "in order to be valid, must be reducible to the fundamental necessities of production and conservation," reducible, that is, to the "fundamental value of the word *useful*." Bataille, instead, anchored his thought in the cosmic principle that the sun gives away its light and energy without receiving anything in return and that, while this allows for the growth and maintenance of life, most is in excess of this growth and squandered on the surface of the earth or lost into the vastness of the universe. Bataille wanted his readers to hold out the possibility that a similar sovereign generosity fuels human expenditure. He wanted them to understand that our compulsion to find justifications for giving openhandedly arises from a taboo, a social prohibition against engaging in expenditures just "for the hell of it," as Michael Taussig puts it.

The taboo against spending just for the joy and fun, or for the pain and horror, of it takes different forms. Writing in 1933 Bataille was particularly interested in the brand of utilitarianism that arose with the consolidation of the bourgeoisie in Europe and that disseminated as a normative ethos to all parts of the globe with colonialism and capitalism's expansion. With this ethos, a social and cultural sterility set in, according to Bataille, dealing a terrible blow, at least for a time, to festivals and carnivals and other forms of collective revelry. If the bourgeoisie did still accumulate wealth, in a massive cultural shift it now spent it "behind closed doors," only for itself, in "an effaced manner," hiding it from other classes. "Today, the great and free forms of unproductive social expenditures have disappeared," Bataille wrote referring to potlatch-like events and the new supremacy of the bourgeois spirit. But, he went on, "one must not conclude from this . . . that the very principle of expenditure is no longer the end of economic activity."

The need for a functional justification of expenditures took on a particularly rigid form with capitalist labor regimes, which firmly channel the spending of surpluses toward individualized vacations, as Roger Caillois, Bataille's friend and intellectual partner, noted. *Vacation* is a word that denotes the emptying of space and time for resting and recharging our productive energies, replacing the exuberance and jubilation of festivals. It became grim with fascist forms of collectivist euphoria and war filling the void left by the waning of communal experiences and by growing social alienation.

In a footnote, Mauss wrote, "The ideal would be to give a potlatch that is not returned." Bataille quoted this footnote. But soon after, Mauss double backed and wrote, "Normally, the potlatch must be reciprocated." Bataille did recognize that the ideal of unrequited giving is hardly ever accepted as such. Nearly always, an expectation of reciprocity or a need to justify expenditures like a potlatch or a carnival extend even to the givers and partakers, who assign them a function based on sanctioned forms of sociability—solidarity or rivalry, for example—or on local notions of social cohesion and prosperity. But for Bataille, these justifications are only secondary in importance to the reality that expenditure ultimately withdraws surplus wealth from circulation. He radically amplified the implications of Mauss's gift theory by emphasizing that expenditure, as a sovereign act, is never reducible to a function or the spirit of productivism.

If from a certain perspective expenditure is indeed functional—bringing about power, honor, and social cohesion—from another perspective it can be wholly dysfunctional—bringing about recklessness, profligacy, and a movement of exuberance that often not even indigence can disrupt. It can also open the door to injurious tendencies, like corruption, for example, or, as with fascism, to violence, catastrophe, and forms of social dissipation "where the danger of death is not avoided," Bataille notes.

Urban markets like El Hueco and Mesa Redonda present us with challenges similar to the ones that potlatch did in North America a century and a half ago to those invested in a Weberian imaginary of capitalism as a formal, abstract rationality. To resist the pressure by academics, city officials, and the media to think of these markets as marginal or backward is to uphold the possibility of an economy sustained, as Polanyi would say, by noneconomic motives or one that doesn't follow the rules of the state but the rules of society. That economy is premised not on the endless buildup of wealth but on generosity, risk-taking, transgression, and the consumption of resources for and with others. For that, we would have to dwell in the markets' rebuff of status and apparent embrace of its opposite, infamy.

Bataille understood expenditure as the sacrificial loss of material things. In sacrifice, he wrote, "the offering is rescued from all utility." In transgressing the imperative of productivity, expenditure thus removes resources from the profane sphere of utility, creating the conditions to temporarily leave the stipulations of routine and ordinary life and enter the space-time of sacred ritual. But the boomerang effect is inevitable, so in solidarity or rivalry, peace or violence, the dissipation of wealth ultimately binds individuals to other individuals in reciprocal relationships as well as individuals to families and groups, groups to other groups, the human world to the world beyond. It creates an expansive network and a complex sociality that, in the case of El Hueco and Mesa Redonda, is in large part instigated by pirates, contrabandists, counterfeiters, the will of some dead nuns, and the sovereign power of the Lord of Miracles and other earthly forces.

10

Next up is Señor Condori. He looks sharp in his sheeny blue suit and cropped silver hair. He stands behind the podium and, with apparent confidence, grabs the mic. But he utters two words and sounds rather crestfallen, diffident.

—Even with all our problems, after listening to the reading of the Foundation Act of our cooperative thirty-four years ago, we still have among us some of the *compañeros* who founded the cooperative with much emotion. . . . [But] that objective they set, we haven't been able to achieve yet.

Roberto had recently told me that Condori is in trouble. He had led the cooperative in its purchase of a piece of land in Puente Piedra, a populous district in northern Lima that is full of promise for investors. The purchase had a dual purpose: The land is where vendors will temporarily relocate while their centro comercial goes up in the current site, and it is an asset from which the cooperative is certain to profit in the future.

But not long after the purchase was finalized, members of the cooperative learned that they could not build on a significant swath of the new property. Zoning regulations designated this area as a setback from the wide and hectic avenue along which the property is located. Condori, so the accusations go, was duped or lured into paying top dollar for square footage that is dead to commerce. What's worse, this dead space is on the side of the property closest to the avenue's sidewalk and thus to foot traffic, usually the location most coveted by vendors. The sale was a fait accompli. There was no backing out. Maybe it had been an honest mistake? Maybe it had not. Either way, the members of the cooperative are irate, and the old man is the lightning rod for their wrath.

In a raspy, shaky voice, Condori goes on:

—This is the moment when we must continue with even more strength in order to achieve that objective. I exhort and call on all of you, you who are here and those who aren't, to say that only united, like the priest said a while ago, can we overcome a difficulty. And we are on that journey. We have, as you well know, an ongoing project for a new commercial center of El Hueco. Likewise, we have another project in Puente Piedra. While we have not yet realized that, we are on our way to doing so. And with the support from all of you, it will be possible.

He pauses briefly, the shake in his voice finally cracking.

—I'm a little unwell, you will forgive me.

He recovers to announce that following his speech a ceremony will take place where his administration will pay just and deserved tribute to the market's founders, those who are alive, and present them with gifts to acknowledge what "our hermanos" did during that time.

Before leaving the podium, his voice croaky and faint again, Condori apologizes once more and, feeling the need to clarify that he isn't just being emotional, says that his health is failing. He speaks with stifled breath.

—Nevertheless, I have been in every moment by your side. Muchas gracias.

A feeble applause follows. He is the image of affliction as he hands the mic over to the MC. He does look ill and visibly carries the burden of what could be a huge oversight or of having been caught red handed. Roberto was diplomatic on this. He said he didn't know. But are these things ever known for sure? The questions, suspicions, and doubts sometimes linger forever.

The rest of the elders patiently stand in line. One by one, they receive their gift, a plaque honoring their participation in the creation of the cooperative, which is delivered in a velvet-lined medal box. Holding the box open to show their plaque, they each take the mic and speak. Haltingly, they express gratitude and recount some part of the story of El Hueco they know. I record the short speeches, but only the words of a couple of them are discernible later through the ambient chatter and the banter taking place around me, which gradually rise to a crescendo, a cacophony of jokes, wisecracks, and sardonic comebacks that are in irreverent contrast to the elders' heartfelt remarks.

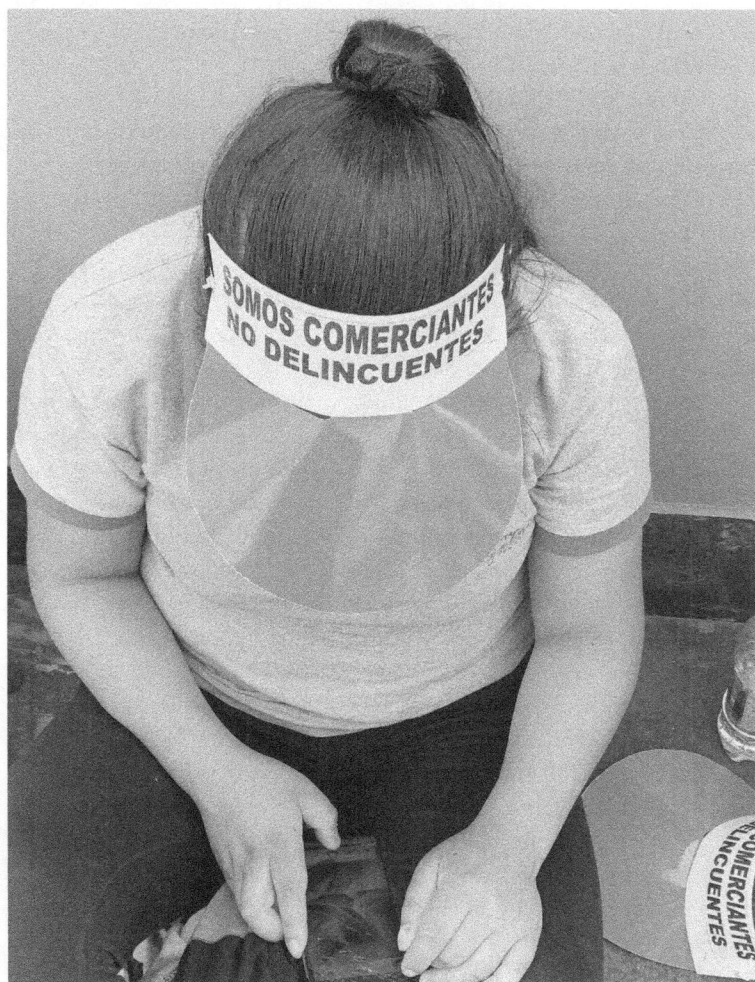

In one of my better recordings, a female founding member says that the cooperative originated at a tiny table and bench on the sidewalk of the fifth block of Jirón Ucayali, another street around Mercado Central. The initial members were skeptical about what good a cooperative would do, she says. But since the police routinely harassed them and confiscated their goods, and the poor souls would cry but never get them back, they thought, "what is there to lose?" She recalls that the objective was for members to obtain a *tienda*, a market stand, so people wouldn't feel sorry for them in the streets. It was Alan García who "took pity" and facilitated the sale of the Beneficencia's property. The woman finishes her remarks and sits back down.

—Alan García! Pffft!

A man sitting near me scoffs. He looks younger than the speaker but still someone who lived through García's dismal first term in office when, amid dire economic crisis and rampant corruption, the sale happened.

Trays with tiny plastic cups of wine begin to circulate among the assembled. It is sweet and amber in color. When only one more elder is left to speak, the MC takes hold of the mic and calls for a toast. He addresses Condori.

—Señor presidente, God willing, may he enlighten you and all your family, give you wisdom, and give you health, señor presidente, as well as strength to conduct this cooperative, which isn't easy at all. It's extremely difficult to convince one thousand five hundred heads, one thousand five hundred modes of thinking. . . . And so, I want a just acknowledgment of our president, Señor José Manuel Condori. We know that we cannot applaud because of the drinking cup that we are holding, but as a gesture, let's lift that cup, and hold it there. Please, right there.

The MC raises his little plastic cup, and people get up on their feet and do as he says. Condori takes the mic again.

—Thank you. Thank you, all of you, hermanos cooperativistas. I've always counted on arriving to this moment to toast with you after honoring those who created this cooperative.

He then makes one last attempt at calming the waters of discord.

—That's why, on this special date when we turn thirty-four years old, being so grownup, I want to toast with you and remind you to search for unity. The father here has left us with an extraordinary reflection: Let's leave the gossip aside. As he said just a moment ago, let's build unity. I believe that if we do, we can achieve in a short time the objective we've so many times desired. I toast for the health of the cooperative, for your own health, and for the future project that will soon be a reality. Salud for unity. Salud for peace. Salud for harmony, hermanos. Let's not live fighting!

The MC takes over and encourages the crowd to a moment of camaraderie.

—What we never thought to do, we are doing today. Salud for our president!

He bellows, trying to rouse the audience.

—¡Arriba, abajo, al centro, pa'dentro! ¡Buen provecho! Up, down, center, and in! Enjoy!

And he downs his wine.

—Ah! How delicious, señores! A very apotheotic moment, very beautiful!

II

Midday

11

The MC announces with an excited pitch that he has a surprise: The cooperative's very first president has honored us with his presence.

—I ask for a strong applause to receive the founder and first president of our Cooperativa de Servicios Especiales Mercado Central! I'm referring to Señor Jorge Montalbán! A strong applause, please! A just homage!

The MC tries to dampen the mounting noise and elicit the appreciation of the audience, who seems more interested in going on with the chitchatting than in what another aging, sickly looking man has to say.

This is the first time I hear Montalbán's name. Señor Vilca would mention him again a few days later when I returned to El Hueco to visit with him. Vilca is in the footgear business, Peruvian-made leather shoes and sneakers of a design inspired by, if not totally lifted from, famous brands. When I got to Vilca's stand that day, he had just rolled his door open and was placing sample items on a display rack in the corridor, which everyone knows can lead to steep fines. Each shoe was wrapped in clear plastic to protect it from dust or damage.

Vilca's account of El Hueco's beginnings dovetails with Señora Emilia's: the continual threats of eviction from the streets of Mercado Central, the fears and anxieties about having nowhere to go, the good fortune of securing a premium piece of downtown land, the complications to prepare it for use, and the way nothing about El Hueco had seemed destined, and yet there it was, almost miraculously. Vilca was present at the earliest negotiations with Alan García about the purchase of the corner lot. García himself feasted the prospective buyers, he told me, and again after closing the deal at the Presidential Palace.

—With ceviche and everything else. Even whiskey, to the point of getting tipsy.

When Vilca joined COOPSE, the budding cooperative had around one hundred members. It was a huge investment of money and resources to prepare the abandoned pit since they had to knock down the partially built cement foundation. COOPSE had to recruit more members to finance the works and fill up the gigantic space. Hundreds of people, from all walks of life, seized the opportunity and joined the cooperative. Contributions flowed in the thousands of dollars. But the money simply disappeared. Unprompted, Vilca said.

—Jorge Montalbán. We gave him the power as president, but in the end, he misappropriated the funds and didn't do anything. He gave people the runaround and pocketed the money.

According to Vilca, Montalbán kept telling vendors that he was making progress. He told them he had rented backhoes and hired workers to break down the useless concrete, but days and weeks passed and nothing happened. Thirty-one thousand dollars were gone before anything had been done, Vilca said.

—Little by little, no one believed in him anymore. That's when I intervened.

Vilca worked closely with Señora Emilia to push Montalbán out and then figure out next steps. He claimed to have made her president, as an obvious trace of regret ran over his wrinkled face.

Señora Emilia didn't steal anything, but when vendors fell behind in the payment of their dues, Vilca said she would pressure them to sell. This is how she got several family members to buy stands at El Hueco. As Vilca spoke, and I took notes, I thought that, of course, I have no way of corroborating any of this or getting Señora Emilia's side of the story now that she is gone. But the story does confirm that even before the market officially opened its doors, the relationships among founding members, including Señora Emilia and Señor Vilca, had already soured and become mired in suspicion and bitterness.

The excavations to level off the ground did, eventually, get underway. Vilca pulled some photographs out of an old, battered shoebox on a shelf. The photos were from the day that, amid toasts with beer, the vendors broke ground. He recalled that it was soon thereafter that workers stumbled upon an old burial.

—A dead person. Her bones. Maybe a nun. Who knows?

Montalbán walks to the front and receives his plaque from Condori. He poses for a picture and grabs the mic. I see Vilca watching from the second row. Montalbán is short and big bellied, and he dons a tan suit that is tight around his distended waist. Merely standing there seems an exertion. But his voice booms over people's private conversations when he begins his grandiloquent, florid speech. He has a soft lisp, and at times his breathing is labored. Amid the flights of lyricism, his remarks take a dramatic turn to address the reality of a shrinking founding-member cohort.

—Many of our hermanos have already left. When ruthless death closes their eyes forever, their memory lingers in our minds, clearer than the midday sun, whiter than snow, sweeter than the perfume of flowers.

He then makes an allusion to the ongoing strife and accusations of corruption directed at Condori and urges vendors to keep the faith and trust the leadership to succeed in what, until now, has been a miscarried enterprise.

—Thirty-four years waiting—he laments—but this year another life will begin, another way. . . . I also apologize to you that in thirty-four years we have had to work in an area of a meter fifty. That cannot be. . . . This year that has to change. But I do tell you, not a cent will flow from here. It will go to your piggy bank and not ours. Enough, neighbors! I have reviewed everything and, about that, I can tell you that this has not . . .

Montalbán wheezes, gasps for breath, and gets unsteady on his feet. His voice dips and the next words are unintelligible.

— . . . in our cooperative!

He rallies to finish exaltedly by invoking "divine providence" and exhorting vendors to lift and help one another so they can achieve their collective goals.

12

Some drink their wine like a tequila shot. I and others do it in small sips. The toast and Montalbán's remarks over, I prepare to slip out the market's side entrance. I have an appointment at the archives of the

Sociedad de Beneficencia de Lima a few blocks north. A filler between events, the wordless melody of a karaoke machine, plays up in the balcony. As I walk away, a man begins to sing, endearingly out of tune, to the familiar track spewing from the speaker. It is "Ella y Él," a popular 1980s ballad by José Luis Perales. I didn't think much of this run-of-the-mill song back then, but today I am unsettled. The lyrics are disturbing. The singer mouths the words like it is oh so normal, like it is the natural order of things.

> Ella se pregunta dónde irá
> Él está seguro de su amor
> Ella le esperará hasta el amanecer
> Él tendrá un pretexto que contar
> Y ella lo entenderá, ella lo entenderá
> Porque sólo vive para él
> Él nunca le dirá, él nunca le dirá
> Que buscó el amor de otra mujer.

The sweetly crooned lines about a gaslighted and subservient woman who complies and endures follow me up the stairwell. The number of women who are street and market vendors in Lima is more than double that of men. So, at El Hueco, I am surrounded by women, but there is an undeniable male-dominant vibe. I am not aware of any woman president in the history of the cooperative besides Señora Emilia decades ago, when its numbers were small. I once asked Señora Viviana at her lingerie and underwear stand why this was the case. Why were there not more women in leadership positions? She replied:

—It is because women do not work well.

Señora Viviana was tending to two stands that day, her own and her brother's, who had recently bought an industrial machine to make socks, and his new business was growing. Her brother's manufacturing shop is in the neighborhood of Canto Grande, faraway from El Hueco, and so Viviana had taken over the management of both stands. Very capably, if you ask me.

The dimness of some corridors together with the content of the stands can add up to an uncomfortable atmosphere for women. I remember early on in my fieldwork walking around the market to get acquainted and finding myself amid a crowd of men at a DVD stand all focused on a mounted TV screen before I noticed the X-rated character of the film. Those DVDs used to sell like hotcakes at El Hueco. Realizing I was the only woman in the vicinity, I scuttled away, my heart galloping with fear.

As the gullible woman of the ballad irons the man's pants and answers the phone for him—as the "Ella y Él" lyrics go on to say—I emerge on Abancay. To my right is Jirón Puno, one of the main entry points to Mesa Redonda. The galerías and campos feriales of Mesa Redonda take up several square blocks between Jirones Puno, Inambari, Cuzco, and Andahuaylas. The sprawling emporium takes its name, synecdochally, after a tiny and crooked alleyway at its very center, Jirón de la Mesa Redonda. In old Lima the names of individual city blocks grew out of the presence of a particular office or church or another notorious feature: the location of a potter's shop, a mule pen, or a traveler's inn. Juan Bromley says that some blocks had names that residents found insulting or undignified—Perros, for example, or Lechugal. All the streets of old Lima were so narrow that on a map they looked like *jirones*. *Jirón* means shred, as in a ribbon-shaped shred of fabric. So, when in 1861, the city decided to modernize the street names, the term *jirón* was adopted in lieu of *calle* and used to rename consecutive blocks along the city grid in a geography-themed pattern honoring the country's interior provinces, regions, and major rivers.

I am surprised Abancay is blocked to car traffic. A crowd packs the wide avenue. Police tanks and officers in riot gear are in standby. Buses and microbuses seem stranded in random places, like they were forced to suddenly come to a standstill. A teachers' demonstration is taking place. Over everyone's heads float signs with the places of origin of each contingent of teachers. I see the Ancash contingent. The one from La Libertad. The massive demonstration, which follows a national teachers strike, is led by Pedro Castillo Terrones. Castillo Terrones is the head of a breakout branch of SUTEP, the Sindicato Unitario de Trabajadores en la Educación del Perú, the old and powerful teachers union. He has been commended for leading an effective teachers strike, and this would eventually catapult him to the presidency of Peru. After a year and a half in office, however, his polarizing and corrupted government would unravel when he attempted a coup d'état without the support of the military on December 7, 2022.

Dodging the crowd and police tanks are bicycle carts with heaps of fruit. They maneuver up the avenue as I cross toward Jirón Lampa, also circumventing demonstrators and police, who huddle around Parque Universitario under the shadow of the Superior Courts.

At the foot of the tower, I am under a stone-carved panel of what look like neo–pre-Hispanic motifs. The interlocking rhomboids in high relief are mesmerizing but strike a discordant note with the spare modernism of the building. Through a tall glass door, I see a piece of a social-realist mural by Teodoro Núñez Ureta: an outsize boy with stretched arms standing on a freshly plowed field while a man, I presume a teacher, hands him a shovel and a book, symbols of hard work and an education. The cinematic tableau pulls me in, but I am stopped at the door by a security guard. I don't have time to stand in line for a swipe of my DNI, my national identity card, so I turn back.

I step down the building's black-marble steps where an *escribano*, a man with a typewriter, is ready to quickly fill out official forms for a fee. Today, he is an index of intractable bureaucracy more than illiteracy. Next to him are vendors of stationary, pens, folders, and paper organizers. Never mind them or the Formica reception desks inside. The building's architectural ambition shines through the drabness of officialdom.

President General Manuel A. Odría (1948–1956) commissioned the project to Enrique Seoane Ros, a Peruvian architect. Seoane's final sketch includes the inversely symmetrical twin tower that is missing on the other side of Abancay. The concave structures form a semicircle around a rotunda that would funnel car traffic through the intersection. The only completed tower was inaugurated in 1956. Its central body

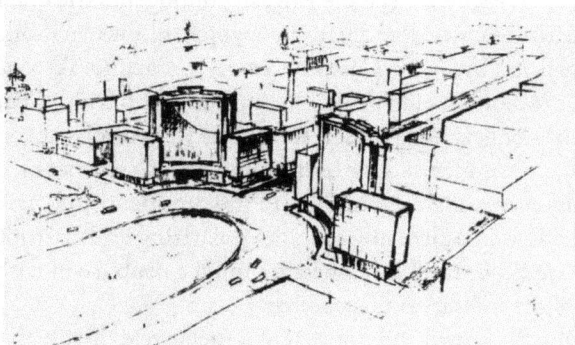

boasted the first steel structure in Peru, flanked by two shorter wings of reinforced concrete, on which the stone-carved panels rest, one facing Abancay and the other Nicolás de Piérola.

I once read that pleasing Odría—whose main aesthetic principle was that verticality was masculine and horizontality feminine—required countless drafts. Seoane's design thus privileges the vertical line, and the building stands out in downtown Lima's skyline among a medley of Beaux-Arts, neocolonial, and other architectural trends. In the 1990s, when the Ministry of Education, which was housed there, relocated to another district, the tower was turned over to the judiciary.

It is difficult to categorize Seoane's ideological allegiance. He was never a member of the modernist Agrupación Espacio but was influenced by it. The collective advocated for Lima's modernization through an urban planning agenda, that, according to their 1947 Le Corbusier–inspired manifesto, would produce the "genesis of a new man," with modernism as the vector of progressive change. The conservatism of the neocolonial and neobaroque styles in vogue at the time, by contrast, were an "anti-art" aligned with the interests of the upper classes. Against these ornate, reactionary styles, modernists vowed to abandon all decoration and accessory detail as "mystifications" of the past. The proposed "new man" would shed all class identity and historical memory and would be liberated from tradition.

Seoane's acceptance of these modernist principles was evident but never total. He therefore never fully abandoned decoration, a feature of his architecture that, in the case of the Ministry of Education, manifested in those relief panels and murals that can be admired from the sidewalk and that infuse traces of local history and tradition into the rational spirit of modernity. It seems Seoane wanted to have it both ways: to take up the Eurocentric progressivism of the International Style, with its humanist aspirations to equality and simultaneous concessions to authoritarian power, while giving a nod to the anticolonial essentialism of the Peruvian *indigenista* vanguard.

Soon after the inauguration of the ministry tower, the foundation pit for the second tower, already dug out, was abandoned. I was about to find out at the Beneficencia's archives that it would be, inexplicably, left empty for the ensuing several decades.

13

On Jirón Carabaya, a short way up from Plaza San Martín and its neo-baroque arcades and slightly martial airs, is the Beneficencia de Lima. It resides in an 1890 Beaux-Arts mansion. A wrought iron entry gate and transomed door give onto a high-ceilinged vestibule supported by dark wooden columns. A set of clerestory windows lets in a gentle light, amplifying the room's penumbra. At the center of the vestibule is a marble replica of Lorenzo Bartolini's *Charity the Educator*. The floor has marble tiles that gleam after more than a century of wear. It is an elegant but at this point lackluster mansion chastened by time. Charity holds a baby in her arms and looks down at a young boy who leans on her leg while reading from a paper roll. Signs of Peruvians' aspirations for universal education and of the sector's perpetual crisis are everywhere—the teachers strike, the imposing former ministry building, the Núñez Ureta mural, and now *Charity the Educator*.

I leave my DNI at the front desk and proceed down a corridor toward the back of the house. I run into a wrought iron spiral staircase that I later learn was designed by Gustav Eiffel. Behind it, two heavy wooden doors lead me into the archives, where I have come for the files that might allow me to piece together some more of the history of El Hueco's millionaire property.

The archive room is dark and cavernous. Floor-to-ceiling stacks with worn leather-bound volumes fill the room. The archivist is in a lab coat. He has a limp and slowly moves up and down the stacks. I fill out a form and make a rather symbolic payment for research privileges. Asked to wait, I pass the time staring at the old parquet floors, which remind me of my grandfather's office on Jirón Camaná. He was born and raised in downtown Lima, where he worked his entire adult life. I remember the flight of stairs up to his second-floor office, sunlight warmly pouring in and landing in long stripes on the parquet. By the end of his career as a lawyer in the 1970s, many offices and businesses had already left the center, the main arrival point in Lima for immigrants from the interior of the country. Those office and commercial buildings were left to age and deteriorate.

I am taken aback. First it was the Seoane tower, with its elegant line and intriguing detail, inducing in me a passive admiration for the

aura of permanence it radiates. Then it was Plaza San Martín. I have
no particular interest in this plaza, but no one can deny its magnetism
as the spatial locus of people's sovereignty. Inaugurated in 1921, on the
centenary of our independence as a nation, it has since been the historical gathering place for political demonstrations. Mayor Andrade
rebuilt it in the 1990s alongside other downtown spaces. His project
to recuperate the center unfolded under the motto "Lima, the way it
once was." I met Andrade around that time and asked him exactly what
historical period in Lima he wanted to bring back. He answered that
it was the Lima of his childhood. The Lima of his childhood was, of
course, Odría's Lima. It shocked me then that such a nostalgic, wistful
stance could have motivated so radical and ideological an overhaul of
the city center. And now it is the mansion and parquet floors at the Beneficencia that spark in me a kind of melancholy about an irretrievable
time in my own life. Are these reactions, mine and Andrade's, what the
modernist architects derided as mystifications of the past?

The Seoane tower is aesthetically interesting, but it was built at a
time of brutal repression. After being treated with the indifference afforded to the recently outmoded, as Walter Benjamin would put it, it
has just been declared Patrimonio Cultural de la Nación. This intima-
tion of the past, however oppressive, as utopic is also palpable at the
Beneficencia. A plaque says that, in its early days, it was home to divorced women with children, some of the outcasts then of conservative
Lima society. The sixth block of Jirón Carabaya where the Beneficencia building is located was in fact called Calle de Divorciadas. But the
charity now runs a site museum to sentimentally commemorate the
institution's history. Andrade was from Barrios Altos. I am from Miraflores. We share a class background that is right smack in the middle
of Lima's middle class. How do these theatrics of history produce in
people like us not a feeling of rejection for the tyrannical reality those
spaces represent but rather a sensation of childhood homesickness?

The air in the archive has the peppery smell of mildew. The shelves
hold documents since before the Beneficencia's creation in 1834. In
addition to sheltering divorced women, the charity managed any social safety net there was for the poor, single mothers, orphans, and
"wayward children." The wealthy donated money and properties for
the Beneficencia to fund its social programs. Later, in the twentieth
century, homes and buildings abandoned by well-off families fleeing

downtown were often turned over to the Beneficencia. Today, it runs state-funded hospitals for the indigent, orphanages, and homes for the elderly as well as Lima's main bullring, Plaza de Acho, and two cemeteries, the historical Presbítero Maestro and the modern El Ángel. In 1968, the year of General Juan Velasco Alvarado's coup d'état, the Beneficencia was brought under the purview of the central state. This is how, in the 1980s, vendors of El Hueco could buy the corner property by order of the president. In 2018 management of the charity reverted to a private supervisory board that now runs it with the input of Lima's municipal government.

A deep voice brings me out of my absorption.

—Por acá.

The next hour I spend reading and photographing a pile of dog-eared pages documenting the ownership of the property from the republic's early years, when the Beneficencia came into possession of it, through the twentieth century. On this first perusal, I gather that, in 1826, five years after the country's independence, a supreme decree ruled that religious orders could only have one convent per city or settlement. It also ruled that convents with less than eight remaining residents had to close and surrender their properties and assets to purposes of instructional and public beneficence. It was under this decree that the last of the Santa Teresa nuns, along with the members of other convents and monasteries, forcibly ceded their downtown properties. Convents in Lima were large landholdings, and whiffs of an urban modernization resolve were already in the air. In 1868 the demolition of Lima's baroque peripheral wall began. The desire for open, Parisian-style boulevards was linked to visions of an enlightened Lima. Wide Avenidas La Colmena, later renamed Nicolás de Piérola, and 9 de Diciembre, or Paseo Colón, built along the traces left by the old wall, were inaugurated in 1898.

If the documents at the archives do shed some light on the history of El Hueco's real estate, they also have a way of deepening the mystery of why, after the last remnants of Santa Teresa came down, the land was never again rebuilt. In 1940 the idea to expand Jirón Abancay took hold. The Beneficencia ceded pieces of the former convent to the city for that purpose. A 1941 report says that the convent and baroque church were slated to be demolished for the expansion, but work wouldn't start until 1947. In 1959, and again in 1961, with the Ministry of Education already looming over the abandoned foundation pit, the president of the Beneficencia writes a letter to the minister of hacienda and commerce claiming ownership of the rest of the property. The charity argues that it was "seized" from them by the central government in 1953 and "occupied" since then without a proper juridical procedure. It is the charity's intention to put to use its primely located property to help the financially ailing institution with more income. The hacienda and commerce minister responds that the Beneficencia can resume full possession of the property any time since construction of the "Banks of the State" projected for the spot was canceled in 1958. No explanation is given as to why this project was discontinued.

Time warps. I read again: 1958. It strikes me as not so long ago. But then it does when I realize I wasn't born yet. It seems unthinkable that the hole of Abancay, a huge, open pit in one of downtown Lima's busiest intersections, has been there for that long. In 1958 Lima hadn't fully undergone the demographic explosion it would experience for the next few decades. The population of the city—which today surpasses ten million, a third of Peru's total—was less than two million. Many people then still held on to the idea of downtown as seigniorial, the most prominent, distinguished place to live, work, and shop. The influx of immigrants sped up in the 1950s and 1960s because of new highway infrastructure, the dismantling of the hacienda system, and droughts in the south of the country. It would drastically transform the city and, eventually, shatter its prevailing self-image of a privileged and distinguished postcolonial center.

But the 1950s and 1960s brought about not just demographic change. They were also years of spatial and infrastructural expansion. Growing up in Lima, I remember learning in school about Odría's vast program of public works, which he carried out over his Ochenio, his eight years in power. Taking office through a coup d'état in the wake of World War II and ruling through the Korean War, Odría benefited from a spike in the global demand for raw materials—sugar cane, fish meal, and cotton—which led to a boom in revenue that financed perhaps the most notable state and public service buildings and housing projects in the history of Lima. The expansion of Avenida Abancay was finished under his purview. In 1953 the price of the commodities tumbled, and although Odría and his successor Manuel Prado Ugarteche (1956–1962) cut down on public spending, the rate of growth of Lima pressured them to continue a robust infrastructure agenda.

Through the governments of Prado Ugarteche and Fernando Belaúnde Terry (1963–1968), who was an architect by training, new ministry buildings went up along with public schools, working- and middle-class public housing units, dams, and roads. All through this period of intense building, and through the twelve-year military government that followed, the hole of Abancay remained.

Architect Fernando Bryce, in a 1966 memo written on behalf of the Department of Works at the Beneficencia, details a proposal to sell the property or build a "great commercial building" on the site, propitiously located in front of what he calls "the future Plaza Castilla"— presumably another project for that juncture that was never realized. Then, a 1978 letter by the Beneficencia's president to Lima's mayor lets us know that neither of Bryce's ideas was taken up. The president says that "for a long period of time" the property had lay vacant and, as a result, been turned into a "public latrine." He informs that in order to contribute to the beautification of the spot, the Beneficencia has rented out space in the outer, street-level rim for "7 one-story commercial shops" until another project, a "Plaza de la Reforma," could begin. But in 1978, Velasco Alvarado's dictatorship (1968–1978) had ended after the coup of a rival general, and the process of a return to democracy was underway. It is safe to assume that the plan for a Plaza de la Reforma on the troubled site was dead on arrival given Velasco's ousting and the tepid success of his reforms, which the plaza ostensibly aimed to celebrate. Two decades later, in 1997, the chief of the Beneficencia's legal department, charged with summarizing the property's ownership history, produces a memo in which he refers to it as "el denominado 'Hueco de Abancay'"—"the so-called 'Hueco de Abancay.'"

The hole was unoccupied for forty-five years. After the restitution of democracy in 1980, it outlived the armed conflict, hyperinflation, the decline of the city center, and the economic and housing crises that flooded downtown with vendors and that pushed its rising population out to new, autoconstructed barrios in the city's periphery built under substandard and often precarious material and legal conditions. An article marking the sixty-year anniversary of the inauguration of the Ministry of Education/Superior Courts tower ends with the following note: "It was painful to learn that the engineers of the project were planning to build another edifice of similar dimensions in front of this one but only managed to leave ready the basement. The work could not continue for lack of interest of successive governments." For lack of interest. A vague phrase that does not clarify much.

When I walk out of the Beneficencia's archives, I am in possession of an abundance of evidence that circles around but never quite pinpoints the reason the hole was abandoned for so long. Considering this void of information, my mind turns to the role the disgruntled nuns and their activation of a tellurian power against all architecture may have played on the fate of this corner property. Was Odría's and Seoane's statist, modernist expression of Peru's "new man" stopped in its tracks by ghosts? Cursed and eviscerated into the unseemly Hueco de Abancay?

I take a shortcut through Jirón Apurímac, a slim passageway that lands me on the back side of the Courts tower. The facade in the rear is a semicircle of beehive windows that grows like a mushroom above the squat block. Around the corner, the teachers demonstration has cleared, but the car and microbus traffic is not restored yet. The fruit carts and other itinerant vendors now move freely about the avenue, their voices blasting over megaphones.

—¡Mandarina! ¡Rica mandarina!

The vendor drags the *a* vowel. ¡Maaaandarina! The singsong rings in my ear as I reach the corner of Nicolás de Piérola and get lost again in the chaos of sidewalk life.

14

From a certain angle, the juxtaposition of modernist tower and hole is a perfect Benjaminian dialectical image. There are the material traces of the past in the building's architectural formalism, expressive of a bureaucratic rationality and iron-fist authority, in tension with the autoconstructed, deforming reality of El Hueco. The clash between the two exposes the mythic quality of the twentieth century's progressive aspirations.

There have been unauthorized uses of space in Lima since its foundation. But in the mid-twentieth century, when the city's footprint blew up, this became evidently threatening of the status quo. José Matos Mar's 1984 book *Desborde popular y crisis del Estado* preceded de Soto's *El otro sendero: La revolución informal* by two years. Written from opposite sides of the political spectrum, both books treated the period between 1940 and the mid-1980s as a watershed moment: The open defiance of the, until then, slow-growing confines of the city looked nothing short of an overflow of people, and the disrespect of its social, political, and bureaucratic norms struck as a veritable crisis and revolution. The space of the city proper as well as its housing stock, public safety and law enforcement, justice system, and public services—schooling, electricity, water, and sanitation—were far exceeded and subverted, and pirate alternatives to these sprung up unobstructed. Unable to respond, the state apparatus had to adapt to the new reality even though this meant its further erosion. In downtown streets and in the autoconstructed barrios of the city, the bitter fights to resist government eviction had all the marks of a class struggle but not one like the one the Shining Path promoted. Opposition to regulation was, for de Soto, *el otro sendero*, the other path, surely also a path of action and confrontation but one led by a business-oriented and rather politically erratic subproletariat that neither Matos Mar nor de Soto could confidently name. In a few decades the millions on this alternative path of struggle reshaped the structure of city government and Peru's entire legal apparatus, and they did so potlatch-style by subverting the forms associated with bourgeois decorum, rationality, and moderation.

Matos Mar sparely used the term *informality*, which he noted had already been adopted by the public. To him, it meant the rebuffing of the "established order," both of the prevalent social and moral norms and of that which is legal, official, or formal. But de Soto made the term central to his book and offered its most concrete and lasting definition. He said that informality is the use of "illegal means to satisfy essentially legal objectives." The term's genesis, however, must be traced back to Max Weber's theory of capitalist rationality. Weber argued that capitalism requires what he called a "formal-legalistic" bureaucracy that "can be counted upon, like a machine" to ensure all operations are calculable and predictable. Half a century later, the term informality arose via a reasoning of this sort: If economies that depend on a legal bureaucracy and recruit labor on a regular basis and for fixed wages can be said to be formal, then, by extension, those economies and types of labor not organized in this way must be informal. It didn't take long for the formal-informal binary to take hold, coming to represent two supposedly distinct sectors of the economy. But the more attention the binary received, the more inadequate it proved to be to explain what really goes on in economies of the global south and cities like Lima. Today, many academics wholeheartedly reject the binary as well as the term informality. They do so on different grounds, including that the latter's value is only relative and depends on the presumed existence of its opposite, a formal economic sector that fully abides by forms and in relation to which it is the inferior term, distinguished by a lack, by the fact it wants for form. But what exactly is form?

In a 1987 economic dictionary entry, Keith Hart says more about Weberian form: Form is "what is regular, predictable, reproducible, and recognizable . . . the presumptively invariant in the variable." He adds that what we call "formal economy" and employ as a point of reference for informality is what we consider to be recurrent and stable, such as the institutions of the modern state, the corporate levels of capitalist organization, and the instruments and concepts with which we study and represent the economy. Saying that something is informal, in other words, is a way of indicating that it eludes those institutions, instruments, and concepts. Informality is that which is "irregular, unpredictable, unstable, even invisible," writes Hart, but it does not exist as such in any empirical, measurable way. It is simply what we cannot command or represent with the tools of normative organization.

If the formal-informal binary is only intimated in Matos Mar's book, de Soto cements it in the imaginary of Peruvians. He first argues that informality is not a static sector of society; it is what people do—their deeds and activities—when the costs of abiding by the law outweigh the benefits. But in his desire to positively capture what he calls the "zone of penumbra" of informality, de Soto reifies the binary into what, by his own account, are two fictional groups of people: *los informales*, whom he puts at the helm of the revolution against the formal order, and *los formales*, who ostensibly belong to and work to uphold that order.

These terms, however, strongly work against the argument de Soto so doggedly develops in the book that Peru has never really had a capitalist economy or a formal legal system. In de Soto's description of twentieth-century Peru, which could be extended to the corruption and scandal-filled 2000s, entrepreneurial success is dependent on political favoritism and bribery. Laws are often crafted in response to private concerns, which creates regimes of exception that engender autonomous little worlds operating legally outside of the law. Examples in the city are vendors who secure a spot in the street by paying a special "tax"; real estate developers who are allowed, ex post facto, to formalize an illegal property; or, with the exception of the one branch of the Tren Eléctrico and the Metropolitano bus system, Lima's entire public transportation network. In the areas of law production and enforcement, in other words, initiatives that move toward Weber's formalism collide with all kinds of particularistic claims, demands for concessions, and private interests that work to deform them.

Thinking back to the journalist who stated that El Hueco "should not be there," his contempt stems not from an assessment of what the market lacks but of what it is and what it does. El Hueco offends. Its defiant attitude and disagreeableness are an affront that brings down everything around it, unhinging the formal-informal binary with "an explosion of affective potential," as Denis Hollier might put it.

Modernist tower and hole, together, are neither formal nor informal but something else, something other. *"Formless,"* writes Bataille, is

> not merely an adjective with such and such a meaning but a term for lowering status with its implied requirement that everything have a form. Whatever it (*formless*) designates lacks entitlement in every sense and is crushed on the spot, like a spider or an earthworm. For academics to be content, the universe would have to assume a form. All of philosophy has no other goal: it is a matter of fitting what is there into a formal coat, a mathematical overcoat. On the other hand to assert that the universe resembles nothing else and is formless comes down to stating that the universe is something like a spider or spit.

15

Jirón Ayacucho is wide and lined with storefronts stuffed with whole-sale packages of Cua Cuás, Doña Pepas, and Morochas: a dreamworld of familiar wrappers of cookies, candy, and other cheap sweets I grew up eating. The city's legion of neighborhood bodegas and candy kiosks come here to stock up. I buy a large bag of Cua Cuás for my son to give to friends in New York City.

I have taken a detour through Mesa Redonda. I am on the south end. Midday, the crowds build up quickly. The road is blocked to car traffic, and vendors and shoppers move about without restriction. A man with a stack of cardboard boxes on his hunched shoulders maneuvers up Jirón Puno. A woman and her toddler son are nearly run over by a hand truck also stacked up with boxes. Three men on lunch break sit on the curb next to a woman and her food cart, their eyes fixed on Tupperware containers full to the rim with stew, rice, and potato. They look at the shaken mom and her boy without seeing them and return to their food. Down the block, a voice issues out of a karaoke machine. Through a rare pause in the throngs of people, I see a woman sitting on the speaker and singing into the mic. She is blind. The sticky melody travels through the air and reaches the food vendor's ears, who absent-mindedly hums the tune. A man and a woman donning vests with the logo of the Municipalidad de Lima, the city government, stroll unhurriedly, hands in pockets, watching over the scene. They slowly turn and reveal the words printed on the back of their vests. FISCAL POLICE. No one stirs.

Street vending in Mesa Redonda is illegal save for the few vendors who have one-year permits. Yet the place is a monument to the supremacy of the street in Lima. Its energy is irrepressible and sometimes desperate. Anguish can be fuel. This is what I think when I see a young man selling bottled water out of a soggy carboard box. He stands in the middle of the road. His sales pitch betrays a Venezuelan accent. He is sweating. He has a vendor of windup fuzzy chickens to his right and a potter selling handmade plates and pots to his left. Other vendors use their bodies as perches for their wares. They all congregate in Mesa Redonda for a reason. In April 2019 a fire in campo ferial La Cochera, which has burned a few times, resulted in a three-week shutdown of a large swath of Mesa Redonda, and the losses for the period were estimated at around $420 million. Vendors assemble here because of the volume of its monetary transactions—$20 million a day!

The street is king in Lima. Days after that 2019 fire I heard a radio interview with the mayor of the district of La Victoria a handful of blocks to the south. He said, exasperatedly, that itinerant vendors, arguably the most vulnerable of all vendors, routinely rejected his offer of a subsidized stand in the upper floors of galerías in Gamarra, Lima's main hub for the wholesale and retail of fabrics. "The galerías," the mayor complained, referring to the top floors, "are empty." Vendors don't want to leave the streets. They prefer trying their luck on sidewalks and roads even though it is forbidden by law. They expose themselves not just to eviction and merchandise seizures but also, as the media sometimes reports, to "mafias" who are said to extort payment in exchange for protection from (obviously corrupted) city officials. "We are giving vendors stands for free. For free!" the mayor repeated incredulously, and by and large these are turned down.

I lift my eyes toward the upper stories of one galería, and these are not empty. I see through the dusty windowpanes the outline of cardboard boxes heaped up to the ceiling. In Mesa Redonda, where space is scarce, the top floors of buildings, unpopular for vending, are frequently used for the storage of stock. The sight reminds me of what Elias Canetti says about heaps of things like these. He says they are the same as crowds of people; they stand in as their symbol. Canetti has in mind heaps made out of the products of harvest, fruit or grain, but I don't think it matters that the heaps here are of fleece blankets, stuffed animals, and clothes. They seem also to be piled up as compactly as possible, for, as Canetti says, "the more there is of them and the denser the pile, the better." There used to be heaps of fireworks stored around here until the big fire in 2001. Fire is also a symbol for crowds, "of the suddenness and velocity of crowd growth," says Canetti. Both crowds and fire grow and know "no bounds." These likenesses between fire and crowds lead to the assimilation of their images. "They enter into each other and can stand for each other." Vendors may peddle in the streets, operate without licenses, illegally occupy public spaces, fail to pay taxes, bootleg copyrighted content, tamper with goods, and forge famous brands, but it is these packed-to-the-brim, illegal storage spaces that city officials most fear. It is in these where most fires begin and through which they spread from story to story, galería to galería, and campo ferial to campo ferial, aided by their violently flammable contents.

Before the 2019 fire, there were at least five fires in Mesa Redonda: the fire of 2001 and others in 2005, 2007, 2012, and 2017. This list does not include outbreaks that were quickly controlled. The 2001 fire was the most destructive. It is the one against which all other fires in the city are compared. It still features in the collective nightmares of Lima residents, and it is compulsively referenced in coverage of Mesa Redonda. The fire's toll was 277 people dead and 180 disappeared, their bodies obliterated in the conflagration.

16

You can see it as it started, the images brutally raw, in a four-minute video shot from a window across the street: The fireworks spurt in all directions, to the crowded street, to other stands packed with more fireworks, upward to the sky only to land on nearby rooftops and set them ablaze and out in huge balls of fire and smoke. The chain explosion was set off by a vendor's demonstration of a pinwheel rocket that goes by the name of Chocolate.

It was around 7 p.m. on the evening of December 29, 2001, two days before New Year's Eve and Lima's grandest display of its people's obsession with pyrotechnics. Andrade, the mayor who had recently evicted thousands of street vendors from around Mercado Central, was still in office. He had requested a national police line to cordon off Mesa Redonda as a way to enforce a fireworks ban in the area. But gradually, the police line grew thinner and then disappeared. Gossip surged, including the rumor that the fireworks vendors had handed out a $100,000 bribe. The recipient of that bribe was left to conjecture. When members of the unarmed municipal police went in to fill the gaps in law enforcement, vendors beat them up with sticks. With no one to secure the area, fireworks made it into Mesa Redonda by the truckloads, turning the cluster of old city blocks into what a weekly magazine described as a "powder keg."

A man who was there that night heard the deafening first blast. It was not quite like a bomb explosion. Back then, people still remembered what a bomb going off in the city sounded like. It was more like a rattle, as if hundreds of iron spokes were being dragged on the asphalt. Following the blast, a panicked crowd ran toward Abancay, where the bumper-to-bumper rush hour traffic sat impassive, nowhere to go. Fire truck sirens wailed in the distance, finding no entry point into the slim jirones, which routed the fleeing stampede of people and cars. In one instant, the air became unbreathable.

A sort of slippery sludge covered the asphalt. A vendor helping others to evacuate warned, "This isn't mud, it is human fat." It is said that, in the chaos, people were mugged. Men ran away with purses, watches, and glasses grabbed straight from people's faces. Then, the electricity in the area went out as the fire reached a power station. Tales of looters prowling in the vicinity spread, prompting fleeing vendors to turn on their heels and run back to their stands, many locking themselves inside with their stockpiles of toys, clothes, New Year's Eve party supplies, and, as firefighters were shocked to find later, more pyrotechnics. Others ran away with boxes of merchandise, including fireworks, in what a health minister's report later called a "suicidal attempt to save them."

At the peak of the fire, there were multiple chain explosions. One swallowed a line of cars parked along a sidewalk. A firefighter who finally made it to the scene said that vendors fought him for control of the water hose. "We were practically assaulted by some [stand] own-ers" who "tried to snatch the hoses to go put out the flames in their own locations." Another firefighter said that the kind of fire that ig-nited that night wasn't quite typified. It spread not just by conduction or contagion, he said, but also by air, lighting up rooftops in faraway places. About 900 tons of fireworks blew up that night. The tempera-ture surpassed 2,000 degrees F.

A few days and again hours before the Chocolate rocket went astray that December 29, vendors had put out two fire outbreaks with buckets of water and *chicha*, a maize drink. The magazine article called the fire that followed "a fire foretold." People's fascination with fireworks, de-spite the dangers and prohibitions in place, points to the ambivalence fire provokes. Caillois notes that while the free manipulation of fire is forbidden, we like to avail ourselves of it anyway. We fear fire but also desire it. Fire attracts and repels the way that all tabooed things do. For Gaston Bachelard, the prohibitions around fire are a mark of the respect we are taught to have for it since childhood. "What we first learn about fire is that we must not touch it," he writes. And thus, "the problem of obtaining a personal knowledge of fire is the problem of *clever disobedience.*" When fireworks blew up that night in 2001, lighten-ing the dark skies above Mesa Redonda, the holiday multitude mistook it for a sign of celebration before the shocking reality of vendors' clever disobedience set in. Most recently, there have been two fires, in 2021 and 2024.

Bataille viewed such "a fire that utterly destroys" as sacrificial and emblematic of his idea of expenditure. Hence his interest in the pot-latch, with the destruction of wealth by fire very much included. Pot-latch helped him reframe political economy with consumption front and center, for a society's surplus "must be lost without profit," he wrote, "must be spent, willingly or not, gloriously or catastrophically." The distinction between willing and unwilling losses or glory and ca-tastrophe isn't always clear. Potlatch-like events are part festival, part sacrifice, and can result in what Bataille describes as "hecatombs of property." Expenditure blurs the line between glory and catastrophe again when it takes the form of mass death, blood sacrifice, or war. In the landscape of Lima, does this mean that Mesa Redonda, with its recurring fires, is some kind of sacrificial zone? A part in the whole of the city doomed to violent consumption?

I turn onto Jirón Cuzco on my way back to El Hueco and pass by the site where the 2001 fire began. Under the destroyed buildings, the blaze had exposed the Huatica Canal, an ancient irrigation channel that was part of a complex pre-Hispanic watering system that allowed trees and fruit orchards to thrive in the desert landscape of Lima. Survivors and relatives of the dead pushed to turn the site, featuring the canal ruins, into a commemorative park. But the park did not last five years before it was swallowed back up into the real estate madness of commercial buildings. The site is now a brick-and-mortar galería that sells paper goods. Everywhere, tall heaps of paper are stacked one next to the other. There is no indication that this was the fire's point of origin, not even a plaque. I try to ask the galería's private security guard if the building is indeed where the fire started. But the guard interrupts me.

—¡No!

The neon green of his security vest blends with a tower of neon-green paper next to him. A flash of tension fills the momentary silence.

—Not here—he says categorically—no fire here at all, ever.

I walk out and see a sign on a third-floor window in the galería next door that reads

FOR RENT
STANDS
STORAGE SPACES

17

Back inside El Hueco, a set of tall, ornate votive candles glimmer in front of the Lord of Miracles. The purple-and-gold wax burns and smokes and collects in thick puddles on the ground.

It is time for the Lord to return to his case atop the ramp. A group of men moves to the front. At the ring of the bell, they lift the platform up to their shoulders. The MC stands near the hovering image and directs the porters to raise it a little higher on one end, lower on the other, to even out the heavy weight. A woman sings the Hymn to the Lord of Miracles into the mic, begging for his blessings, as vendors come and touch the platform with the pads of their fingers before crossing themselves. Others clap as the Lord exits the courtyard.

The singer's gauzy, plaintive voice fills up the space:

> Señor de los Milagros
> A ti venimos en procesión
> Tus fieles devotos
> A implorar tu bendición

The painting of the Lord at El Hueco is a smaller replica of the official one kept at the Convent of Las Nazarenas a few blocks north. Every October, the image at Las Nazarenas is the protagonist of the largest procession in the Americas. The canvases, both at El Hueco and Las Nazarenas, are oil reproductions of an image of Christ crucified said to have been painted in 1651 on an adobe wall by an enslaved "Angola" man. History books and lore explain that the wall with the image miraculously survived, intact, the devastating earthquakes of 1655, 1687, and 1746. For this reason, this Christ is also known as Señor de los Temblores—Lord of Earthquakes.

I watch as the MC locks him in his case. The Lord now looks out from behind the glass. I had been visiting El Hueco for months, if not years, before I paid any serious attention to him. When Señora Emilia first told me that the Lord of Miracles was El Hueco's patron saint because he was effective against the property's cursed soil, averse to all construction; when I first learned that vendors had invested significant resources in upgrading and maintaining his altar; when I heard, skeptically, that in October the massive, citywide procession of the Lord of Miracles sometimes stops by El Hueco to meet the market's devotees, I was hearing what people were telling me but was not quite listening. It wasn't until I learned about Odría's failed modernization efforts for this downtown spot that the Lord's entanglement with El Hueco's history piqued my interest, and his ascendancy, as enabler of the market's present, moved from the margins of my awareness to the center.

Much of the power and authority this New World Christ accrued over the centuries came from its association with native Pachacámac, the mighty pan-Andean deity of earthquakes. For the last millennium before the Spanish conquest, Pachacámac's oracle and shrine, located in the valley of Río Lurín south of Lima, was the most important *huaca*, or sacred site, in the central Andes. In the early years of the conquest,

the administration of the valley went to a conquistador who owned property in Lima. He brought a group of Indigenous people from Pachacámac to work for him in the city. As a result, that part of Lima where these laborers settled to live and work has since been known as Pachacamilla, little Pachacámac.

The Lurín valley underwent a near demographic collapse due to violent displacement and disease. But in Pachacamilla, the group of

Indigenous workers endured, commingling with enslaved Africans owned by the conquistador in a kind of symbiosis, says María Rostworowski, that set off a special transformation phenomenon by which Pachacámac became a dark-skinned Christ. Around the painted Christ of Pachacamilla, as he is also known, the cult of the Lord of Miracles gained force through the seventeenth century as protector of Lima against earthquakes, its sovereign power linked to native Pachacámac who, as the *anima* or soul of *pacha*, the earth, could both unleash and restrain them.

The first chapel for this Lord was built in Pachacamilla, sheltering the wall with the original painting. His worshippers included the growing number of Africans and Afro-descendants in the city, whose devotion deepened as earthquakes destroyed churches and homes and knocked down the chapel's roof but not the wall with the painting. The wall came into the purview of the Convent of Las Nazarenas, today located along Avenida Tacna, which was established by royal decree in 1771 on the site of the old chapel.

The cult of the Cristo Moreno—the Black Christ, which is another of the Lord's names—and the Black brotherhoods that formed around him, were officially banned for much of their early history. But worshippers' celebrations continued clandestinely, which moved church officials to try to destroy the cult, something they obviously never achieved. The Cristo Moreno's power was feared both for its links to Indigenous tellurian forces and the hybridizing spirituality of his Black devotees, who reportedly began their rituals following proper Catholic form and ended them with their own, African-inspired forms of praise. But if these feasts offered a reason for the cult's repression, they also made it more public, adding to its popularity among what was known then as Lima's plebeian classes. Based on censuses of the time, historian Alberto Flores Galindo explains that the city's pleb was grouped into four categories of people: servants, artisans, enslaved people, and "vagrants." This last category comprised itinerant vendors, who wandered in the streets, plazas, and church atriums of Lima and who suffered from a bad reputation because of the unfair competition they posed for storefront retailers as well as their lack of scruples about paying taxes and the sale of substandard, contraband, or stolen goods.

The votive candles flicker in front of the void that remains after the Lord's departure, and I am left to wonder about the subtle, elusive alliance there is between him and the new plebeians of El Hueco in their resistance to the city's regulative authority and urban planning ideals.

18

I pull out my copy of the anniversary program. Roberto gave it to me when he invited me to come. It is a glossy foldout leaf with El Hueco's logo on the front. The logo features the double-pine-tree motif of the American cooperative movement. On the back is a photo of a barren landscape. A white perimeter wall surrounding the vendors' new property in Puente Piedra stretches into the distance. In large, block lettering, the wall says that the future Centro Comercial El Hueco II will soon open there.

The program lists the upcoming events. Some have sponsors, vendors whose gifts will bankroll them. Among these are a "lunch of camaraderie" and a number of artistic performances. A note accompanies them: A kind donation of so and so. It spells out the donors' full names. No pretense of modesty or anonymity. There is a separate list with more donations that also includes the givers' full names and amount of money or beer they have contributed: a total of 4,685 soles—about $1,300—and twenty-six crates of beer. The program's centerfold is busy with loud promotional pictures of the bands and the dance troupe whose acts are planned for after the lunch, which, the program says, will be enlivened by Brisas del Perú, an Andean folk music band.

The chairs in the courtyard have been rearranged into a wide circle. Whiffs of sautéed spices reach those of us lingering near the chairs in a holding pattern, awaiting lunch. I notice that some vending stands have opened. Their roll-up doors are collected at the top, and their wares are displayed on racks and hangers along the corridors.

I walk down a tunnel of balloons. Some mannequins, cut off at the waist and with overly pronounced buttocks, exhibit pairs of super tight blue jeans. Fake Adidas and Nike jogger pants and shirts hang amid unlicensed Disney and Marvel merch. The corridors become quieter and sparser near the edges of the market, farthest from the entrances. In the area where stands used to sell pirate and homemade pornographic DVDs there is now a Bibles and Christian books and videos section. This change came in the wake of scandals and arrests related to reported sales of porn involving minors and rape videos. On the south end is the largest section for the wholesale and retail of pirate CDs and DVDs of more suitable content. El Hueco has for decades been a well-known source for these, perhaps the main one in Lima. It supplies para-ditas and campos feriales throughout the city. Given the decline of CD and DVD formats for media storage and playback, there are now new delivery mediums for pirate content, such as preloaded USB drives. It is also possible to custom order these to one's specifications. While the old disc stands have scant decoration, as if trying to pass inadvertently with a spare aesthetic, the USB glass counters ooze a velvety, LED glow. I am not the typical buyer. My gaze is met with curious eyes and body language. Vendors keep a wary vigilance for strangers. Their copyright infringement of content from all over the world also makes them the target of recurrent seizures. They are the reason behind some of the longest shutdowns El Hueco has endured.

It is difficult to keep track of all the police interventions. A newspaper estimates that between 2002 and 2014, there were about eighteen, some of them followed by closures that lasted as long as a month. There have been at least as many since 2014 for reasons pertaining mainly to piracy but also to infractions of the building code and civil defense and the trading of illicit goods, that is, more porn, contraband cell phones, bootleg sneakers, and brand-forged, expired, or controlled medicines. The year 2014 was particularly busy. There were four raids by the fiscal police: the first one in June for piracy; the second one in July, when the minister of the interior himself showed up; the third one in October with the participation of the minister of production, when more child pornography was allegedly found after a police contingent pushed its way into the market. According to the president of the cooperative at the time, they did so while shooting bullets at the ceiling to intimidate. Finally, the fourth one was in November for vendors' failure to comply with commitments they had made to address safety violations. In this intervention, the police built a brick and cement wall blocking the entrance and preventing vendors from going in. Given the market's steel double doors, this was a totally unnecessary but effective stunt that TV news programs made sure to broadcast.

In fact all these police raids made for flashy news headlines. The market provokes both fascination and outrage. One thing is the battle that El Hueco and other poorly or unregulated markets, as transgressors of the law, wage against law enforcers. A completely different thing is the battle they wage in the realm of politics and public opinion. From 2011 to 2014, the head of the Office of Control and Inspection at Lima's municipal government was a media and politically savvy official named Susel Paredes, who today is a congressperson. There are a dozen videos online of the first 2014 raid where she took turns speaking to several news outlets. In one video, with the shuttered stands visible on the edges of the screen, members of the fiscal police have dumped sacks of confiscated CDs, DVDs, and empty plastic cases on the cement floor, making an enormous pile in front of the cameras. B-roll footage shows a steamroller driven over the brittle plastic to destroy the goods. It shocks to see hundreds of thousands of soles wrecked. The made-for-TV moment is meant to exhibit Paredes's unbending, total authority and maybe also to dispel suspicions of corruption—the police seizing the discs and selling them themselves.

Paredes declares into a reporter's mic.

—This is material voluntarily handed over by the vendors of El Hueco, who are fourteen hundred, but there are two hundred that sell pirate DVDs. For two hundred, we are not going to harm twelve hundred wholesome vendors who sell clothes, appliances, who give out receipts, who abide by the law. So, what we want is to pull out a rotten tooth in a mouth where all the other teeth are good.

The reporter picks up the DVD of a popular Peruvian film from the discarded pile and notes that it was pirated and sold at El Hueco before it was released in theaters. The cooperative president also appears on screen. He is just two months into the role and seems overwhelmed. His demeanor is one of full compliance. He steps up toward the mic and speaks with his eyes fixed on the ground. He refers to Paredes as *jefa* and *doctora*.

—I am indeed committed to eradicating this [piracy]. As the doctora says, because of a minimum number of people, the fifteen hundred associates that work here cannot be negatively affected, and that is the pure truth.

A news anchor back at the studio asks Paredes why the city allows El Hueco to exist at all given that it "is an authentic hole." His voice exudes derision. But with her folksy style, Paredes is quick to skirt both the question and the reporter's disparaging language.

—I believe that repression is not a sustainable solution. If I only go after, pursue the itinerant vendor, and I confiscate from him, he'll pop up again elsewhere. If I transform him, I will solve the underlying problem.

In subsequent months and years, the raids continued. In a 2017 operation, also well choreographed for the cameras, viewers see nearly twelve hundred police officers and thirty-four prosecutors descend on the market early one morning. Susel Paredes and her down-to-earth, convivial style are gone from city government, and in contrast to the subterfuge of amicable collaboration, this raid is a veritable show of force. The market, inside and out, is flooded with police. Those in full riot gear pose in formation, several lines deep, while the fiscal police tramp up and down and force open the stands suspected of trading in pirate goods. In one of the many videos of the seizure there is loud banging, it seems the sound of sledgehammers hitting the security padlocks. The police haul away hundreds of bright yellow garbage bags full of confiscated material.

The anniversary celebrations and the festivities to observe other holidays as well as the leisure trips, games, and contests that populate El Hueco's yearly calendar might seem to be occasions at odds in spirit with the raids leading to closures and the impounding of goods. The first are joyful, the second punitive. But they in fact have a lot in common. The feasts and recreational activities, like the seizures and shutdowns, in the end amount to major expenditures of vendors' wealth and productive time, to the profitless use of their resources and even their sheer destruction. The pace and rhythm of life at the market is equally punctuated by these two kinds of interruption of its ordinary temporality.

The edginess in the pirate corridors is as tangible on this anniversary day as ever. But I am aware these stands aren't the only ones still taking risks. In a recent raid, the police confiscated a batch of alprazolam, a controlled substance, that was illegally dispensed out of a stand selling bags, purses, and backpacks—what for Paredes would qualify as "wholesome" goods. It turns out that it isn't easy to set apart the rotten from the good teeth.

19

A prayer to the Lord of Miracles is printed on the first page of the program. It pleads to him to listen to vendors' entreaties and supplications, to give them faith and hope, and to free them from egoism and evil. "Most holy Lord, forgive our sins," it reads. "Amen." On another page, in an acknowledgment, the cooperative's administrative council expresses gratitude to those who have generously given their moral and material support to make the anniversary day possible. It then beseeches the Lord again to pour his holy blessings on each and every one of those donors.

Vendors ask a lot of the Lord. To move him to respond, to prompt him to be generous, most are his devotees. They keep his altar clean, endowed with fresh flowers, and they make him the centerpiece of their feasts, bringing him out of his glass case and parading him down to the courtyard. They pray and supplicate to him, even if not everyone with the same intensity. Señora Viviana once admitted in a hushed voice that she likes the Lord of Miracles but is more devoted to the Virgin of Sorrows because she cured her of a serious illness. Nevertheless, community resources, to which Viviana and everyone else in the market contribute, are sacrificed to don the Lord with paraphernalia worthy of his status. But even if, as Mary Douglas writes, "sacrifice is a gift that compels the deity to make a return: *Do ut des*; I give so that you may give," everyone who lavishes time and resources on the Lord knows that reciprocation is never assured, that it always hangs in the balance.

Bataille explains that gifts are always losses in potential. In bestowing a gift, we always take the risk of not getting anything in return, not even recognition. He says that gifts are beyond calculation at some point. This is why expenditures in the form of gifts, favors, offerings, donations, and bequests take on the visage of a sacrifice. Secretly, maybe even to ourselves, Bataille says that we give because we want "to go beyond the narrow limits" within which we live and which govern our existence; we want to transcend the realm where our actions are justified only if they are a means to the ends of productivity and usefulness. Sacrifice is unpredictable. It is the opposite of production to secure the future. In sacrifice, we experience the now, the present moment. We rescue the offering, and through it ourselves, from our condition of things and our subordination to labor and utility and future-oriented projects. This is the source of the exuberance, of "life grasped in its intimacy," that comes about with expenditures that go beyond the limits of reasonableness and calculation for returns.

But if giving wealth away openhandedly, like many vendors do, stems from a desire to restore life to the movement of exuberance and to a state of intimacy with the world, and if we stake a part of ourselves in doing so, this is also the basis for the ruse, what Bataille calls "the comedy" of the gift. We want to go beyond the limits of calculation and reasonableness but at the same time feel compelled to "bring our going-beyond" back within those same limits for a reward. We want to be, as Bataille says, unlimited and limited at the same time. Vendors give away freely, but their names must be noted in the program for recognition, and thus the gifts take the meaning of an acquisition. This is "the gift's power, which one acquires from the fact of *losing*."

Right outside the pirate CD and DVD area, I see the tower of beer crates waiting to be tapped. It is in full view, impossible to miss, as if on display. Such a gift is a two-way street in that vendors make sure it is known in what direction the blessings and the credit must travel. It is also an ostentatious way to remove wealth from circulation, like sacrifices do. The individual and collective munificence will be expended in the joy of good food, live music, and dancing and drinking into the night.

20

Brisas del Perú begins to play on the balcony. Today it is only one man and his guitar. The first tune is a slow, melancholy *huayno*. It is beautiful. The chatter quiets down. A somber, intimate mood takes over the expectant crowd.

I think of Octavio. I imagine a young, upstanding, middle-class but rank-and-file corporate employee waiting on hectic Abancay as his fuming boss descends into the hole. From a certain perspective, El Hueco is just a market, a workplace like countless others, made up of regular people with regular lives, joys, and sorrows. But from Octavio's perspective, it is also a place that demands we contend with what, from the standpoint of political economy, are excesses and transgressions, such as vendors' proclivity to flirt with the forbidden, their defiant outlook toward the law, the avoidable win-or-bust gambles they take, and their expenditures that, while justifiable as gifts that give back, flout the premises of rational accounting for reinvestment and growth. These excesses, which often betray a nothing-to-lose attitude, few theories of the so-called informal economy account for or assimilate into their logic.

De Soto's *El otro sendero* was written to be a book with commercial appeal. It directly spoke to the middle classes, who were grappling with the brusque transformation of their city, as well as to the poor, working, and immigrant classes, who, through the book's well-publicized arguments, learned that their businesses, homes, tastes, ways of being in the city, and indeed their very persons were "informal." The book argued that since the 1940s, immigrants had arrived in Lima by the millions, full of energy and ideas, only to find no jobs and endless hurdles to their business initiatives. This was because Peru did not have a capitalist but a mercantilist economy, closer to the one Spain had imposed in the sixteenth century. This meant that lawmaking catered to the powerful with a plethora of particularistic and contradictory norms that made running a legal business absurdly costly and impractical. It was against this mercantilist system, with its networks of privilege and tangled web of laws, that, according to de Soto, los informales had mounted a capitalist insurrection. But their revolt cut two different ways: If los informales had revolutionized the status quo through "a succession of millions of acts," that is, millions of transactions outside of regulations and the law, they also opened a breach through which most other Peruvians were following suit. Trying to adapt, the state had conceded too much to the offenders and undermined its own relevance.

The book's vivid descriptions of economic life in Lima, both optimistic and anxious, made it extremely relatable for local readers. But its argument that the defiance of norms and regulations was a grassroots expression of the capitalist spirit inside the common person became the center of core debates in Latin America and the global south. One of them had to do with the relationship of informality to criminality.

For de Soto, los informales violated the law but only as a means to lawful goals. Smuggling electric rice cookers into the country is illegal, but trading and using them is certainly lawful and legitimate.

By contrast, other forms of illegality are antisocial and even criminal, such as the sale of tampered medicines since their consumption could be lethal. So are drug trafficking, thievery, and terrorism, and these, de Soto clarified, were beyond the scope of his analysis. Alejandro Portes and other sociologists of the so-called informal economy, who share de Soto's belief in a teleology of progress and development, also posited that "a key distinction must be made between informal and illegal activities."

This makes sense since they believe, in Weberian fashion, that bringing nonregulated businesses under the control of a merit-based, technocratic bureaucracy is crucial to achieving an advanced and prosperous economy. But markets like El Hueco and Mesa Redonda show that parsing out the harmless from the antisocial or criminal isn't quite doable or realistic in any practical or theoretical sense. Hart and Matos Mar knew this.

When Hart, who is largely credited for coining the term *informal economy*, was doing field work in Accra's neighborhood of Nima in the 1970s, he observed that the income opportunities residents relied on in their daily lives ran the gamut. Intertwined with on-the-books wage labor was an improvisational and creative pulse of life that overflowed with an excess impossible to reduce to categories: Income sources included farming, shoe shining, the off-the-books sale of all kinds of legitimate goods, the sale of stolen objects, smuggling, sex work, bribing, "middlemanship" in courts of law, and corruption. Illegal didn't necessarily mean illegitimate since, in Nima, ingenuity, trickery, and rule-breaking rarely resulted in disgrace. They rather enjoyed a kind of legitimacy and were vital for access to many sources of income. Thus, Hart saw no point in excluding them from his analysis. Matos Mar's take on the street economy of 1970s and 1980s Lima, which he characterized at its core as *contestataria*, or anti-establishment, also included clandestine, illegal, and criminal actions and operations.

This difference isn't only definitional. It stems from diametrically opposed understandings of what the economy is and how it works. In the Weberian imaginary of capitalism, economic decision-making excludes social values and tradition (the ritual, magical, and supernatural included) in favor of an impersonal formalism and "a rationalistic economic ethic." In contrast, Polanyi said that economic behavior is always submerged in social relationships and institutions. Traditions and cultural attitudes are intricately implicated. The repercussions of this observation are expansive. People experience legal regimes and bureaucracies based on their social standing. We cannot ignore that, historically, those regimes and bureaucracies have been instrumental to colonial expansion and plunder. Following Polanyi, both Marshall Sahlins and Lomnitz affirmed the social embeddedness of the economy, where, as Lomnitz says, local rules of sociability and obligation can have an "almost 'sacred' character." Lomnitz discusses the ways informal networks of reciprocity operate in society and *within* bureaucracies based on kin, friendship, loyalty, and trust, and they lead to dispensation of privileges that range from mere influence to services and favors to bribes and other forms of corruption. Lomnitz writes that "personalistic, culturally determined loyalties to kin and local groups often defy the more nationalistic ideologies that underlie bureaucratic rationality."

When we speak of millions, as we do of the populations of big cities, Canetti says that the abstract number becomes filled with a "crowd-meaning." De Soto did write about immigrants as crowds, multitudes, armies, and legions. But he also wrote about immigrants as individuals. The city individualizes, he argued. Immigrants were citizens in the making who based their actions not on whim but on a rational assessment of possibilities offered by the city. In this light, immigrants were no longer a strange and tumultuous crowd but an emergent and vigorous new class of people, not wage earners but entrepreneurs. In an apparent jab at Marxism's notion of a "reserve army of labor," the unemployed and underemployed on which capitalism depends to keep wages down, de Soto referred to los informales as an "entrepreneurial reserve." Los informales were entrepreneurs operating in the zone of penumbra out of necessity and against their will. To claim this and frame himself as the champion of this new socioeconomic class, de Soto had to exclude arbitrarily all socially and legally questionable activity. He had to isolate the good, productive, and reasonable informal, who breaks the law for efficiency and self-improvement, from the bad, criminal, and harmful informal, whose behavior is antisocial or antisystemic—lumpenesque, as Octavio put it about El Hueco's vendors.

❉

III

Afternoon

21

A man and a woman, at the pace of a couple out window-shopping, come down the ramp holding hands. Another man, this one with a sweaty brow, comes behind carrying a large cardboard box on one shoulder. They go across the edge of the courtyard glancing at us with only a glint of curiosity.

Suddenly, there is a quickening in the crowd. From a narrow stairwell between two stands descend a few women with plates of lunch on a tray. They hand them out to people sitting in the circle and rush back up for more. I get a plate. Feeling like an interloper, I look around for a more entitled person to get served first. No one takes the plate from my hands. Mine is a gesture that elicits a predictable response from a neighbor I didn't realize had noticed me.

—Eat, please.

Everyone eats with gusto. The cabrito, yuca, and rice is delicious. The whole cabrito has gone into the stew, and I get a piece of meat on the bone and a piece of entrail. I grew up eating entrails and used to love them, but the texture and flavor feel barely familiar in my mouth after decades living abroad. My neighbor is a young man with wavy black hair slickly combed back and a button-down shirt under a V-neck sweater. He turns to me again:

—Sabroso, no?

I nod and ask if he is a cooperative member. He is not. His name is Josué, and he is the cooperative's manager, an employee. He volunteers that at El Hueco people are "good believers."

—They leave aside their conflicts and come together in the Lord of Miracles—he tells me.

It is clear Josué knows who I am. But how does he know so precisely what I am interested in?

Roberto approaches and pats Josué on the shoulder.

—Provecho—he says.

The expression means something like "may the food nourish you." Roberto turns to me.

—Come up by my tienda when you're done.

He leaves, and Josué goes on.

—The older generation tends toward its roots. If you convene them to an event, say, to a carnival, they do their part, especially if it relates to where they are from. *Al toque*, right away, people sign up. From Cuzco? Pum! They collaborate. From Puno? Pum! They donate to it. The rest follow their example. For today, the cooperative handed out the balloons, but everything else was donated.

I sense Josué feels an affinity. He is a fellow outsider looking in. I am intrigued by his emphasis on *paisanaje*, on the commitments immigrants in Lima make based on a common place of origin. Paisanaje is the source of forms of reciprocity and cooperation that also sustain life in the Andes. While those networks are critical when a person first arrives in the city, the exigencies of running a business eventually interfere with these place-based ties. Paisanaje is thus retooled into what some call *asociatividad*, a strategy where individuals from different walks of life join forces to create associations and cooperatives whose purpose is to advance shared economic goals or other causes that run the gamut from securing property rights to advocating for better state services to improving neighborhood life. Today, thousands of associations and cooperatives are inscribed in the public registers. With a legal personhood, their mission is multiple and fluid and ranges from self-defense to mutual aid to political brokerage.

The young priest's broad allusion to common origins during the mass tells me that an ethos of paisanaje is still somewhat alive at El Hueco, but only once has it featured in my conversations with vendors. I was visiting with Señora Emilia one day when a man came to request her help to persuade a popular priest to officiate a mass for his market association's patron saint. She told me she would help him because he was a *paisano* from the same Andean town where she was born. But asociatividad is much more prominent today, with its aspirations to harmony and cohesion, expressed, as in so many towns across the country, in the devotion to an adopted patron saint. These patron saints, according to Manuel Marzal, suggest themselves to devotees and potential devotees through their dreams, miracles, favors granted, and promises made, and they create "a mythical space of shared solidarity." I cannot speak to how deeply this devotion runs for anyone individual or how universally it is felt in a particular community of vendors, but it certainly is a coalescing force in the tempo of social life and the use of material resources in markets. If saints are benevolent and can take care of problems, as Señora Emilia hoped with the Lord of Miracles, they are also intolerant of indifference. They expect to be feasted—honored with a mass, a procession, food, dances, and fireworks—that is, in a celebration that signals, according to Marzal, a "rupture between the festive days euphorically lived and the rest of the year dedicated to work."

Josué and I eat to the last grain of rice on our plates. When he is done, he gets another plate. All who want seconds get them, and we all eat to our heart's content as the guitarist regales with his sweet, sorrowful voice.

Josué gets up to leave. On his chair is a crumpled copy of today's paper. On the front page I see a story about a galería whose building burned down two months ago in the commercial emporium of Las Malvinas. Vendors from the galería, the article says, were let into the building in small groups to search for possessions that might have survived the fire. They came back out crying. Nothing is left to rescue. All burned to ashes.

That nothing is left to rescue is obvious if you stand in front of the ruined structure. I was there last week. It takes up a whole block, the walls of the building now a patchwork of exposed cement and charred paint. All the glass is gone from the windows. On the rooftop are the calcined shells of prefabricated metal enclosures that had been illegally erected in the building's airspace. The day of the fire, four young men worked inside of one under lock and key—a common practice, the press said, to stop workers from stealing. Their job was to forge the brand of cheap lighting fixtures by replacing the factory logo with the fake one of an expensive brand. The building's upper floors were used as storage spaces, and word is that the fire began with someone soldering near a stash of paint. The flames spread in a flash. As the fire raged, the locked-up workers stuck their arms out of the barred windows and filmed themselves with their phones: "It's all over," they said in the recordings as they realized they would not be rescued. The article says the fire is under investigation.

Before I go up to see Roberto, I tear out the page with the story and put it away inside my notebook.

22

Abancay is the usual racket of rumbling engines and honking horns when I pop back up to the street. The morning humidity, which should have lifted by now, lingers sticky and heavy. I walk in the wet air to Roberto's stand along El Hueco's peripheral wall and soon my sweater is damp. Roberto rents this stand from the cooperative, but he owns another one inside that he rents out to someone else. I find him with his back to the street, his head stooping over a box of custom picture keyholders, mementos for a baptism. He is placing each of the objects in a little plastic envelope before he delivers them to his customer. His business engraves this kind of commemorative keepsake for family occasions and business events. I always find him in exactly this position, hunched over some job he must quickly finish. He shoots me a look from under the visor of his cap.

—¡Hola!

He keeps working, and we seamlessly fall into conversation. Roberto trusts me, for some reason he always has, since the day we met. This surprised me. I had gotten used to the apprehension, a skittishness pervading every encounter in this zone of penumbra, as de Soto calls it, where people like to be visible and invisible at the same time. Maybe Roberto's transparency has nothing to do with trust or with me. He behaves as if he has nothing to hide. I open my notebook and place it on the glass vitrine where he is working, and he begins to talk. Roberto habitually raises his voice over the commotion of buses and microbuses outside as they creep up the avenue.

He works mechanically, his fingers disconnected from his thoughts, while he tells me that they are almost ready to launch the next call for building contractor proposals. They have finally gotten over the last imbroglio. The ad hoc committee last charged with writing the terms of

reference for the bid had done so with one company in mind. What's more, the project requires two professionals on payroll: one architect and one engineer. Those terms of reference asked for three and required bidding companies to document experience with at least five similar projects, which is perfectly unnecessary. The process had all the marks of bid rigging. To stop this from happening again, a jury of vendors will supervise the new process, Roberto tells me. He is cautiously optimistic.

—Our vision is to formalize. To be competitors, like Metro or Saga.

Metro and Saga Falabella, a supermarket chain and a department store, respectively, are owned by Chilean multinational corporations. Just as they do, Roberto wants El Hueco to take advantage of the TLCs, the Tratados de Libre Comercio, or free trade agreements that Peru has with multiple countries and that have allowed such foreign capital nearly to take over Lima's retail market. He believes El Hueco has the potential to compete by directly importing from China. But that potential is nowhere close to being realized. Roberto gives me an overview of their prior failures. The first project was for a nine-story building, but vendors weren't able to secure financing. The second was for one of eight stories, but no one thought to do a feasibility study. As it turned out, no vendor was willing to go higher than the third floor. The next project had only four levels but no storage spaces. A redesign of this version of the project to include storage spaces was voted down in general assembly because of the cost. But the design for the fourth project is already approved, Roberto tells me.

—The problem is our distrust because *dirigentes*, leaders, take advantage. Leaders want to gain for themselves, like kickbacks from suppliers. A leader says to himself, "Me amarro, y la hago." A little quiet double-dealing, and I'm set.

Roberto says he was once a "formal" vendor. His father created the business—back then it was making custom rubber stamps—but it never gave him enough to support his eight children. As a young man, Roberto joined the military and later enrolled in a technical institute, but he dropped out because he had neither the money nor the time to study. He began to help his father sell rubber stamps in front of a bank. Eventually, he took over the business and grew it enough to rent a storefront downtown. He later bought the place, which was set up perfectly for his business. Everything was on the books, Roberto said.

—I obtained my RUS from SUNAT and had my sales receipts. I also applied for a license.

SUNAT is Peru's tax collection agency, the Superintendencia Nacional de Aduanas y de Administración Tributaria, and the RUS is a business's tax ID number, the Régimen Único Simplificado. A vendor who hands out sales receipts is, in theory, a vendor who pays taxes.

Roberto goes on.

—Then officials from the Municipalidad said: "You're missing this, you're missing that, a fine for this, a fine for that." When I placed a sign above the entrance to my store: "Señor, that's forbidden." The real estate company that sold me the store had tricked me into buying a space zoned only for parking. More fines.

He had to shut the business down, sell the space, and go back to the street to sell his rubber stamps.

—If you're informal, nobody comes to bother you. All you need is to begin to formalize, and they come looking for defects.

Roberto took advantage of an amnesty program for people who owed steep fines to the municipal government, but he never acquired another storefront. All this happened in the 1980s during Alan García's first government.

—I was making an exorbitant income. I thought I was going to retire at forty. But I hadn't diversified.

In 1990, Alberto Fujimori unleashed his IMF-mandated Structural Adjustment Program, which severely devalued Peru's currency from one day to another. The New Sol replaced the Inti 1 to 1 million. Roberto's savings turned to naught. He had to start from scratch. In 1996 he joined the vendors of COOPSE, which soon after being expelled from the streets of Mercado Central would be allowed to move into the corner hole.

—Here, I run into the difficulty of shortsightedness. But the reason we haven't fully formalized is *la cultura chicha.*

Chicha, the maize brew, is an Indigenous drink. Chicha, by extension, has since the 1980s been applied to things perceived as urban pastiche of Andean cultural elements. For instance, the popular music genre, also called chicha, combines Andean melodies with electronic instruments. Chicha is most definitely seen as ingenious and innovative, but for many in the city, it is so to a fault since it is oblivious to norms and undeferential to tradition, precedent, and middle-class mores. Roberto defines for me la cultura chicha:

—It is the culture of *Pepe, el vivo*—he says, denoting the caricature of a man who is clever and self-interested to the extreme and always looking for ways to game the system.

We learn to be this way from those in high places. For example, *el Chino* stole, Roberto says about Fujimori who is Peruvian-Japanese but whom supporters and detractors alike call El Chino, the Chinaman.

As long as he did works, everyone was happy. This is, according to Roberto, what people used to say about the former president. That's the level of complacency and general tolerance of abuse. A lot of people accept corruption in exchange for a minimal degree of efficiency. Taking advantage of a position of power is, to an extent, legitimate and thus difficult to eradicate.

Roberto tells me that he has nothing to complain about the current mayor. He means Castañeda Lossio, the former councilman who, back when vendors were on Jirón Huallaga, encouraged them to organize into a cooperative. He is now mayor for the third time. Roberto also mentions César Miranda, the former head of the Formalization Division in the city government, and Miranda's boss.

—They changed the law for us.

By "us" he means campos feriales like El Hueco and those in Mesa Redonda, which can now get operating licenses. Roberto muses as he bags the last few keyholders at the bottom of the box:

—I can't understand the conservative attitude of many here. They have money. They own stands in other places. They want a building, but they want it now. They don't want to invest and wait during the long construction period.

I am writing that down on my notebook—"vendors do not want to wait . . ."—but I stop.

—I want to leave—he says abruptly—the cooperative spirit doesn't work well here in Lima. The idea of the common good doesn't have a hold. Everyone guards their own private interests, defends what's theirs.

A customer walks in. She has come to pick up the keyholders. Roberto pivots to pay her his full attention. I step outside to get out of his hair.

23

I look around: A man sells portraits of Jesus, Mary, and Catholic saints in gold-colored frames on the sidewalk. A small crowd gathers around the demo of a portable sink. It siphons water up from a vat and shoots it out in a jet. It is a clever solution to the prevalent lack of running water in Lima. An old, rusty bus leaves a black plume of exhaust in its wake. It engulfs a woman who is lifting a wheeled cart onto the sidewalk. The cart is loaded with warm bread of different types. I can smell it even in the noxious air. She settles by a beef-heart *anticucho* and steamed corn cart, crowding the sidewalk even more. Now a mouthwatering whiff of the grilled kebab hits my nostrils. Mingling with pedestrians, young men and women, hired hands at El Hueco's street-facing food stands, aggressively shove copies of their menus on our faces.

In the 1970s, before the idea of an informal economy took hold, Latin American Marxists devised the concept of "marginality" to account for the new dominance of this edgy, disorderly way of working and living. It supplemented a vast body of work arguing that the economies of Latin America were peripheral in relation to the capitalism of the west. In those Latin American nations, wage labor proper was in crisis, and as a result, a large part of their labor force was excluded— Aníbal Quijano said "secreted"—from participation in the economy. More numerous and visible than the wage-earning proletariat, this population of nonsalaried workers was a marginalized, new social stratum that Quijano called "los marginales" and José Nun "la masa marginal." The question of what class position these marginalized people occupied became an urgent one since it was difficult to think of a revolution with a protagonist that had no place in the bourgeoisie-and-proletariat class structure.

In Marxism, the "reserve army of labor" is a by-product of capitalism and has a function in it: to guarantee a regular supply of workers under conditions favorable to the owners of the means of production. Latin America's marginal mass, conversely, was more like the lumpenproletariat, which, according to Marxism, plays no role in capitalism or in the revolution against it. Los marginales could be identified not just on account of their large numbers but, according to Quijano and Nun, also on account of their lack of cohesive social identity and the perverse ways they participated in society through "clientelism, criminality, illegal trade, proliferation of ghettos and marginal populations, persistence of brutal forms of exploitation, and so on." If they were inclined to violence, it was not of a revolutionary kind but of a localized or defensive nature.

The relationship between the proletariat as the revolutionary class and the lumpen had also haunted Karl Marx and Engels in the prior century. Hal Draper pinpoints their anxious efforts to separate the two and purify their categories of analysis—political economy, the proletariat, the revolution—from the excesses of the lumpenproletariat (which literally means ragged or rogue proletariat). Draper shows how rhetorically laborious it was for Marx and Engels to theorize the proletariat so that the term was applied only to the sector of class-conscious, wage-earning laborers devoid of lumpen qualities: the declassed, parasitic, volatile, criminal, knave, itinerant, demoralized traits—all terms from Marx's and Engels's writings—that made the lumpenproletariat a nonclass, an excrescence, a monstruous, useless growth in the system.

Marx and Engels wrote about the lumpen with vitriol. They despised it even more than the bourgeoisie. If the bourgeoisie was necessary for the class struggle, the lumpen was made up of unruly elements that exerted a corrupting influence and imperiled the revolution. As the scum and refuse of all classes—again, in Marx's words—the lumpenproletariat was—now in Engels's—a gutter-proletariat. Marx and Engels desperately wanted to set apart the good, productive, and class-conscious proletariat from the bad, rogue, and destructive lumpen, whose behavior is uncivil and antisocial. As much seems to have been at stake in the good-bad, productive-nonproductive distinction for Marx and Engels as it was a century later for Latin America's left- and right-wing revolutionaries, such as Quijano and de Soto.

It is, of course, too simplistic to say that vendors at El Hueco and Mesa Redonda are lumpen in the Marxian sense. They, after all, do produce and even accumulate. But they don't do so like proletarian workers, conscious of their interests as a class. They do so potlatch-style by respecting and then subverting the norms of economic rationality and bourgeois moderation and decorum. They do so, in other words, by pushing the logic of capitalism it to its very limits, often putting everything on the line for short-term gains as with the material losses and grim reality of human exploitation that came out to the bright light during the deadly fire at Las Malvinas. Soon after the gruesome event, the International Labor Organization stated that the men had been victims of a modern form of slavery.

Robert Bussard argues that in Marxism lumpenproletariat never acquired the status of a concept. The term rather elicited irrepressible affect from Marx and Engels and always appeared next to a barrage of insulting, disparaging adjectives that aimed to debase the population it alluded to. That population, which for Marx and Engels exceeded categorization, offended their bourgeois sensibilities, their "middle-class Biedermeier (or Victorian) mentality" and produced in them fear, condescension, and even hatred. It is treated like a formless and useless waste product that cannot ever be eliminated or reassimilated into productive society. Lumpen is thus a catchall term that issues forth as a reaction to social and material worlds that "should not be there," a put-down of members of the working class and the urban poor who do not think, behave, or look as Marx and Engels thought they should.

Vendors at El Hueco do not behave or look as city officials, urban planners, or the media think they should. But while it is indeed too simplistic to say that they are lumpen, they know how to mobilize the affects associated with the term and use them as a resource for a way of doing business and politics that has worked for them so far. Vendors refuse assimilation into the state bureaucracy and to a great extent embrace their reputation as irredeemably antisocial. A structural miscreation, its physical presence in this important corner of downtown disrupts and deforms city planners' ideals while enticing us to their side, inviting us to descend into the depths of their corridors and luring us to also transgress. Could this kind of social and material form of defiance be called, to borrow Rosalind Krauss's phrase, a politics of the lumpen?

As a source of power and a politics, lumpen is thus not a fixed social condition or group of people in the bottom rungs of society. Roberto is clear on this. He thinks we should not lose sight of those in high places. Crucially, Marx decried lumpen behavior also across class lines. In *The Eighteenth Brumaire of Louis Bonaparte*, he hurls lumpen accusations at Bonaparte, whom he hails as the "chief of the lumpenproletariat." He also hurls them at members of the bourgeoisie who, along with the Paris lumpen, had joined Bonaparte's movement. Rather than a fixed social trait, lumpen is a resource that can be appropriated and used by anyone. When Roberto said, "We are, well, a hole!" the comment indicated that if lumpen as a resource opens up important spaces for action, it just as easily shuts others down. Lumpen affirms, defies, and empowers, but it also weakens, coerces, and tyrannizes.

24

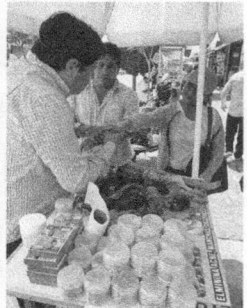

Roberto's customer leaves, and he is on a roll again. When his nephew
walks in, he doesn't so much as give the boy a nod and goes on talking.
The nephew, who is there to help Roberto run the business, enters a
tiny cubicle and sits down in front of a computer screen.

Roberto opens a box of engraved paperweights. He tells me that, of course, he doesn't like paying the fines the city regularly levies for piracy since he has nothing to do with those stands. He speculates why the city comes at them with so much resolve.

—They do it to divide us.

Or, it could be that with the upcoming mayoral elections, someone wants to please the national association of authors and composers by cracking down on El Hueco. Roberto says they have been told that they can sell pirate content as long as it is not from national artists. Law enforcement can feel that haphazard and arbitrary to vendors, who then turn for explanations not to their law bending but to runway speculation and conspiracy theories.

Without ungluing his eyes from the screen, the nephew updates Roberto on the goings-on down in the courtyard.

—Tío, they're gonna give out the prizes now.

Roberto closes the paperweights box back up and puts it to the side.

—Let's go.

In this event, hired salespeople are the protagonists. The MC announces the prizes for best corridor decorations: three cases of beer for the first place, two cases for the second, and one case for the third. There will also be a raffle among all participating corridors for a wine demijohn. The time and labor put into the decorations is obvious, including the astonishing number of balloons, easily in the thousands, which have been manually inflated and chained into all sorts of shapes. I saw salespeople huffing and puffing all during lunch, blowing up balloons. Roberto and I watch the winners jump up and down, hug each other, and walk back to their stands with the coveted prizes.

Señor Anastasio is up in front, applauding and cheering. I find my way to him through the standing crowd. Anastasio is a hardware vendor. His stand is packed with tools, coils of wire, electrical supplies, brushes, and flashlights. He is a serious devotee of the Lord of Miracles and promoter of his cult. He once told me that, in the year 2000, after the Lord had been venerated at El Hueco for a couple of years, he and the other hardware stand owners formed a brotherhood to fund and preside over his worship. The first order of business was to outfit the Lord with a proper representation and a heavy wooden anda worthy of his status. The brotherhood threw a fundraising party and collected

$1,000. Each of the members then pledged 1,500 soles, at the time about $450, and, with the funds, they commissioned the oil replica of the Lord that was paraded earlier today down to the courtyard.

In addition to the oil painting and the anda, Anastasio and the other brothers persuaded the cooperative to furnish the image with a gold and silver frame and a set of silver flower vases. Evoking the language of sacrifice, he told me that they wanted the Lord's altar to "cost us something." But they could not convince the cooperative to buy real gold and silver. Reportedly, the painting at Las Nazarenas weighs nearly one ton and almost half of its weight is real gold and silver, some of it encrusted with real gems. Its frame is also adorned with precious-metal insignias donated by the brotherhoods that manage the citywide cult. The painting at El Hueco is just like the one at Las Nazarenas, Anastasio told me, except for *las joyas*, the jewels. They did persuade the cooperative, however, to create a fund dedicated exclusively to maintaining the altar.

Anastasio tells anyone who will hear about his unshakable faith on the Lord and about the stubborn opposition Pentecostalists put up. They complain about the ostentatious veneration of an image. Anastasio retorts that, at least, Catholics like himself are moved to generosity by their faith, to charity, to donating to the needy, and to trying to make the world a better place. What do Pentecostalists do? Everything they do is just for themselves, for their own gain, Anastasio tells them.

When the MC pulls a raffle number from a bowl, and the demijohn winners walk away with the big jug of wine, everyone claps and some in the crowd tease:

—¡Combida! ¡Combida! Share! Share!

Besides the idolatry, the frivolity, and the drinking, Pentecostalists must disdain the Lord's cult because of his history and trajectory, such as that they are full of mysterious, quasi-magical turns of fate and transformations, from an Indigenous deity into a Black Christ whom the church tried but failed to fully repress and who, conversely, worked his way up to the top of the pantheon of saints and lords. The Lord of Miracles must strike Pentecostal vendors as exceptionally dangerous because of his fusion with non-Christian divinities and forces and the openings this could have created for the absorption of evil—a source of pollution and disease—into his worship. There was a specific event that made the Lord's trajectory irrevocable, linking him forever to the autochthonous powers of the earth.

The event was the earthquake that hit Lima on October 28, 1746. The Port of El Callao, west of downtown on the shores of the Pacific Ocean, disappeared under a tsunami. The levels of destruction caused by this earthquake inaugurated a period known as "the ruin of Lima," which spanned the second half of the eighteenth century and manifested in the fear and dread not just of more tellurian movements but also of violent social unrest against the upper classes.

There were good reasons for this. In the aftermath of the earthquake, massive looting targeted the collapsed as well as the still-standing mansions and homes of the rich, adding significantly to the destruction through the plundering of building materials: wood beams, window frames, doors, and other reusable construction supplies. Having upset the daily rhythms of a tense social cohabitation, the earthquake brought conflicts between classes and castes to a climax. It is important to note that, at that time, Africans and Afro-descendants, whose numbers peaked by the mid-seventeenth century, made up about 50 percent of Lima's residents, with the "Angola caste" as one of the major ethnic groups.

Flores Galindo writes that the term *plebe* had strong derogatory connotations. But, as if it wasn't derogatory enough, it was often qualified with even stronger, more demeaning adjectives and insults, such as vile, lowly, trifling, injurious, and abject. Reading Flores Galindo, I am reminded of Marx's and Engels's lumpenproletariat and of the way city officials and pundits speak about El Hueco, Mesa Redonda, and other poorly regulated commercial worlds in Lima today. Flores Galindo says that the term plebe was flexible; it stretched to encompass Lima's "lumpen world," he says, in an anachronistic reference to the Marxist term, which, for the Lima context, he characterizes as bandits, thieves, and everyone else thought to be connected to "the organization of everyday life at the margins of current conventions."

After the 1746 earthquake and uprising, the Bourbon regime's strategy to recover a semblance of order in the city centered on improving the built environment through architectural projects aimed at reconstruction but also at regulating street life. Churches and other buildings had been used as a form of social control also during Lima's baroque period, but this was done with ambivalence. In 1671, for example, fear of a Black rebellion in Lima called for the reconstruction of the chapel of the Cristo Moreno, but the cult itself was repressed. As the rising popularity of the Lord of Miracles garnered the support of those in power, state-driven architecture and the Cristo Moreno grew to be elements in a double-pronged tactic to keep the pleb in check.

When the procession of the Black Christ through the streets of Lima was instituted as an annual event in 1753, it was as much in response to the fear of earthquakes as it was to the fear of the unruly pleb. Their religious devotion represented the pleb in its best behavior and under control. Viceroy Manuel de Amat y Juniet, known for his contributions to the Bourbon project of ordering the city through public works, cinched the fame of the Lord in 1771 by means of the reconstruction of Las Nazarenas chapel into a church. The hope was this would limit the autonomy the brotherhoods of Afro-Peruvians had to manage the cult and the site of devotion, which Suzy Sánchez Rodríguez says was perceived to be an "extreme space," indistinguishable from the population that inhabited it and that threatened the city's stability.

Up on top of the exit ramp, the Lord of Miracles seemed at first a pristine, uncomplicated counterpoint to El Hueco's rogue underworld. But is it? This impression changed as I learned that his cult stems from Indigenous and African forms of praise and worship that were historically repressed as idolatrous and defiant. It only makes sense, then, that the Lord is now deployed by a group of Lima's new plebeians as a protective and political tool to subvert the state's modernizing vision for this corner of downtown.

25

Eloy rents a stand at a campo ferial in Mesa Redonda. A few days ago, he told me:

—I hope piracy never goes away!

We chuckled at his obviously inflammatory comment, but it was clear he meant it since a good part of his business is the import, wholesale, and retail of supplies media and music pirates depend on. That day, several people came by his stand and made inquiries or bought from him: a box of USB drives, toner for a color printer, a packet of plastic sleeves. Eloy answered their questions, handed out their change and receipt, and returned to our conversation without missing a beat. We got into the subject of corruption. As he stocked a glass vitrine with smartphone cases, Eloy said that he is not into politics, but he was considering running for office at his vendor association. The reason was that its current president is a thief.

—He steals. I would understand if he stole only what's just and did works. But no, he just steals. Stealing is never right, but if someone works hard and steals a little it's understandable.

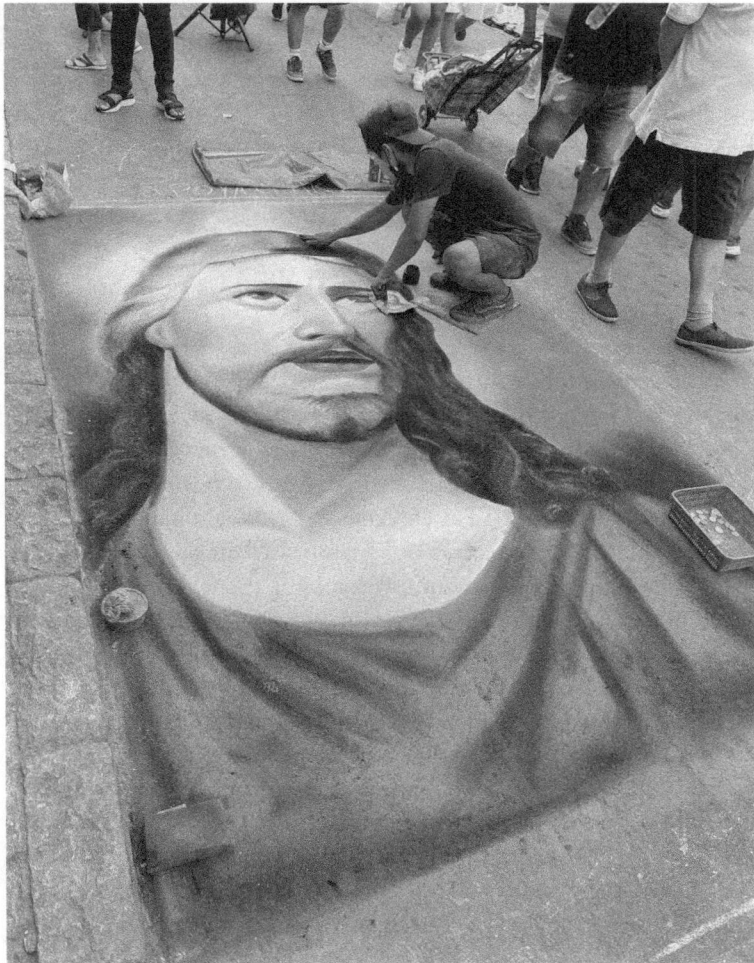

My thoughts flew to Roberto. That kind of acceptance of corruption drives him crazy.

It was not a particularly busy day at Eloy's, and he was chatty. He spoke about being discharged from the army and going to university. He used to be a troublemaker, he tells me, but he has chilled out a lot since then. The only reason he hasn't gotten his degree yet is that he hasn't met an English proficiency requirement. But he hasn't given up. Many people at El Hueco and in Mesa Redonda want to tell me about their frustrated journeys through higher education. They know I am an academic, and the subtext of their stories often is an awareness that I come from a privileged world where such frustrations are less common. I had so far seen or heard nothing other than the perfectly ordinary goings-on at a Mesa Redonda stand when a vendor from down the corridor walked up and spoke to Eloy.

—Can you sell me an invoice like the other day?

I thought, Am I hearing right? They didn't seem to care I was there while they negotiated.

—Paper or electronic?

—Electronic. Can you backdate it?

—Not if it's electronic. Only today's date.

—Make it for five hundred soles. Or, can it be six hundred?

Pirates steal content from creators. Association presidents allegedly steal money from vendors. Are Eloy and this guy also stealing? If so, from whom? A businessman friend tells me later that the buyer of the invoice was probably taking money from his own business by faking a purchase and writing it off as an expense. He would have paid Eloy a smaller sum for the transaction and reciprocated the favor in the future.

As I stood by at Eloy's stand overhearing the terms of the deal, I could not avoid the pitfall Janet Roitman points to in her critique of studies of markets in sub-Saharan African countries. Those studies, she says, assign an outsize role to states and bureaucracies and view those markets in opposition to idealized models, to which they always fail to conform. Weber's would be one such idealized model. This overemphasis on state regulations and their infraction precludes our understanding of how those markets *actually* work in contrast to how they *should* work. At the root of this problem, Roitman suggests, is the received and largely undisputed idea of "capitalist development as unambiguous linear progression and the privileged signifier of modernity."

The markets are thus seen as mere "deviations, dysfunctions, or even pathologies" of those ideal models.

I am painfully aware of this trap and have a sincere desire to understand El Hueco and Mesa Redonda for what they are rather than what they "are *not yet.*" For that, I sometimes have had to ask really hard questions and have learned the hard way that vendors are squeamish when I probe too deeply. They perfectly understand and perceive as threatening preconceptions like the ones Roitman identifies, which policymakers and researchers like me bring with them. I once queried Señora Emilia about the financials of her stand, and she rebuffed me, letting me know I had crossed a line. This was a year before she died.

At Eloy's, as a result, I froze in place and just listened to the exchange with his neighbor. I took at face value that it was an illegal operation, one such deviation from the ideal, as Roitman puts it, and feared that asking him to spell out what it was all about would be overstepping. Plus, Eloy had already shared with me where his ethics lie. He abhors laziness more than anything. Hard work and effectiveness entitle one to certain leeway and legal work-arounds.

Portes, following Polanyi, argues that strong state regulations and controls are essential to capitalism. Without them, markets disintegrate. In contrast, de Soto is adamantly against anything but minimal regulations. Ignoring burdensome ones is part of a sound cost-benefit analysis that is the heartbeat of a self-regulating market. But in the long run, skirting regulations does entail risks and costs that can result in tremendous losses for businesses. He thus advocates for the simplification of bureaucracy and the deregulation of the economy—for barebone laws modeled after the pragmatic attitude and "extralegal" normativity of los informales. Institutions of the state must deliberately do what they are already doing by default and in a haphazard way as they fight to stay relevant: behaving like a "mimetic state" that is becoming itself informal through imitation and contagion.

But organizations like the vendor cooperatives and associations of El Hueco and Mesa Redonda are not models of stability and predictability. They come into being and dissolve, become active or inactive as vendors need them or not to defend themselves before authorities. Their norms are crafted and adopted, valued or ignored, based on the cohesiveness and trust there is among the membership at any one point in time, which is usually low. De Soto knows this. "As a general rule," he writes, "when treated individually [vendors] prefer to disavow their organizations if that allows them to obtain an advantage." "Pragmatic"—the adjective de Soto uses to characterize the attitude of los informales toward their leaders, organizations, and norms—fails spectacularly to capture the shape-shifting and opportunistic quality of such extralegal normativity. Pragmatism is also, arguably, what makes Eloy and so many others so tolerant of illegality. This is the business world in which the Peruvian state, according to de Soto, must find inspiration for its legislation.

In 1990 de Soto became Fujimori's advisor, and a reformist era ushered forth. The reforms included the creation of new state institutions, among them the Fondo de Cooperación para el Desarrollo Social (FONCODES) for poverty alleviation and the Organismo de Formalización de la Propiedad Informal (COFOPRI) for the formalization of de facto occupied property. SUNAT, for tax collection, and the short-lived but powerful Ministry of the Presidency, headed by Fujimori himself, were restructured to be more limber and efficient. The personally run ministry bypassed the bureaucracy of other ministries and agencies to channel the revenues collected through the privatization of state enterprises into public works such as roads, electrification, and public schools, allowing Fujimori to claim all the credit.

Three decades of legal reform following the publication of *El otro sendero*, however, led not to the massive incorporation of Peruvians into the institutions of the state and the law, but to a deformation of any existing formality through the gaps and loops created by legislation driven by clientelism, bribery, and corruption. Fujimori's own corruption, his clientelist use of FONCODES and COFOPRI in the late 1990s to secure votes for his reelection, and the thuggish tactics of his shady advisor Vladimiro Montesinos to intimidate and bribe congresspeople, large swaths of the press, and the entire upper echelon of the banking and entrepreneurial class spawned such expressions among the public as lumpen state, lumpen press, and lumpen empresario class.

This state of affairs has only become more acute in the post-Fujimori era at the local and national levels. Fujimori was imprisoned in 2007 for corruption and the torture and indiscriminate killings of civilians during the armed conflict. He was freed some months before his death in 2024. Three of his successors would eventually also be imprisoned or spend time in house arrest, while another one would commit suicide during his arrest proceedings. All four ex-presidents faced or are facing accusations of corruption. In 2016 Keiko Fujimori, Alberto Fujimori's daughter, lost the presidential election, but her party, Fuerza Popular, obtained 70 out of 130 seats in Congress. Furious about her loss, Keiko vowed to govern through the legislative power, and, under her direction, members of her majority caucus opened up a Pandora's box of vengeful and illegal applications of the constitution as well as of corrupt and opportunistic lawmaking that no one can close now.

Under the government of Dina Boluarte, which is beholden to the whims of Congress, the conservative left, of which Boluarte is a part, and the far right, including Fuerza Popular, have joined forces and legislated to take over the judiciary and the electoral power, disembowel the laws against organized crime, and, as an extension, favor the interests of illegal mining and timber cartels. These activities account for as much as half of some local economies and are linked to killings, including of dozens of Indigenous leaders, and the scourges of human, arms, and drug trafficking, gold and mercury contraband, deforestation, and pollution.

26

A brass band comes down the ramp. It is well outfitted with horns, saxophones, trumpets, drums, and three tubas. The musicians wear sunglasses despite the overcast skies. Each has a red jacket on over white pants and shirt. The band serenades the cooperative with an up-tempo Happy Birthday. Some vendors clap along. Others sit listless and watch. Now they launch into a fast-paced *marinera*, a genre of music that mixes Spanish and Indigenous rhythms, and the MC encourages the crowd to get up and dance. He alternates his exertions, aimed at keeping the mood lively and those in the audience engaged, with calls to members of the administration to join him up in front:

—Members of the vigilance, education, mutual aid, and electoral committees! Come help blow the candles!

On the table that earlier served as the altar are two large cakes. The cakes have green, yellow, and white frosting and are decorated with the double-pine cooperative motif on top. The MC exclaims into the mic and taunts:

—Two lovely cakes, very giant, of course! How delicious the cakes are! If you don't come down, you don't eat cake. It's that simple!

No one from the committees comes down. The MC insists and also cajoles the audience:

—Approach, please! Committee members! Although if you all don't sing along, you don't eat cake either!

In lieu of regular candles the cakes have tall sparklers. Some committee members finally gather around the table, and one of them lights the sparklers. They shoot up bright, sizzling sparks high above their heads.

I wince. Are they really playing with fire in these cramped quarters, with the nylon fabric as improvised ceiling and much else that could go up in flames? I instinctively take a step back, but for many others the sparklers are magnetic, and they move to the front. They get as close to the cakes as they can, swarming the table. I make a video of it and later see Roberto in it, standing on the far end of the packed crowd with a big smile on his face. His arms are lifted, and he is waving to the band, requesting an encore. I can hear his voice booming:

—¡Japi berday! ¡Japi berday!

The band plays a couple more rounds of Happy Birthday, and most people sing jumping up and down. Many of them have been given confetti poppers. They point them up and off they go. Thick clouds of confetti rain as some in the crowd clamor to cut the cake:

¡Queremos que partan la torta!
¡Queremos que partan la torta!
¡Queremos que partan la torta!

I am taking pictures of the confetti showers, the shimmering bits falling in slow motion like in a snow globe, when a text pops up on my phone screen. It is from Hugo Sulca. He is the well-known and respected leader of Galería Nicolini at Las Malvinas, the market that recently burned down. People speak of him as a maverick businessman. I have been looking forward to meeting him, so the last time I visited, I left a note with an associate. Sulca's text says to come by tomorrow or Monday to talk.

The associate I left the note with is Sulca's go-to person. He asked me what my interest in meeting Sulca was. I mentioned the fire, the ruined building . . .

—Yes, it was un fumón.

The associate interjected to say that it had been a stoner, someone lighting a blunt who had provoked the fire.

—Un fumón?

—Yes, he was sent by the competition. The Chinese from down the block, or the Chileans. That kind of thing doesn't happen just like that without the intervention of someone. The real question is who let the fumón into the building?

The spine-chilling Galería Nicolini fire an act of arson? By the market's competitors? I didn't know what else to say, how to carry on with the conversation. Nodding, I wrote down the information on my notebook, thanked him, and left.

When I met Sulca in person the day after El Hueco's anniversary, he was more standoffish on the source of the fire. He said he would rather not say.

—Me reservo.

Sulca is too politically savvy to share what he thinks or to speculate, what with the galería's liabilities—Mayor Castañeda Lossio had come out and blamed the vendors—and the pending insurance claims. He added tactfully:

—I will only say that there are people who are happy with the misfortune of others.

Sulca has a storied life. He hails from Ayacucho and, like the old guard at El Hueco, began as a young man selling in the streets around Mercado Central. He is an outspoken advocate of formalization. Two years before the fire, he decided to persuade stand owners at Galería Nicolini to obtain not just a corporative license as a market but also individual ones for each stand, which is what the city government aspires to for galerías and campos feriales but hardly ever achieves. Sulca had made great inroads, presiding over a tidal change in vendors' views on the benefits to gain from formalization, when he was shot as he was leaving the premises. The opposition to Sulca's project was small but fierce. He had received threats on the bathroom's wall: "Muerte a Sulca" (Death to Sulca). Some vendors loathed the idea of tighter controls over sales of dubious merchandise, such as subpar or knock-off electric cabling.

—That earned me six bullets—Sulca said.

Three hit him in the back and shoulder, and one hit the market's treasurer in the abdomen.

I asked him what would happen now with the burned building. Sulca said he didn't know. He had hired experts to assess the losses, and the experts had found that the building was salvageable. It would only need reinforcements here and there. But city officials had their own agenda, he said. They brought their own experts who said the building must be torn down. Some stand owners had sided with the officials. Sulca was sure they had been bought. He was irate.

When Sulca brought in yet another set of experts, from Japan and from a Lima engineering university, they wrote a report that agreed with the first experts' conclusions.

—The report had one thousand pages. One thousand pages!

But the pressure was on. City officials came around and, in a coercion measure, shut down an extension of the galería that hadn't been affected by the fire. Sulca looked sullen.

—It's all about private interests. People with power and money still rule in this country. That is the problem.

A newspaper article ultimately reported that with the "consensus of 100% of owners and renters" the building would be torn down. How this consensus was achieved, the reporter doesn't say. But after the horrors of the fire—broadcasted on national TV and now imprinted in the blackened, hollow ruin, which, according to the article, had become a den of malfeasance—vendors want it gone. They want to restore their reputation. A mall with a food court, escalators, shops, parking lots, and an auditorium is to come up in its place.

One by one the sparklers on the cake fizzle away. I breathe with relief that none of their emissions went too far astray to set something ablaze. But no one else looks concerned. People erupt in an excited ovation, hooting and howling with pure delectation.

27

Urban huayno pours down from the balcony. A family band—the leader, his two brothers, and his eleven-year-old son, a wunderkind of an electric guitar player—is now on. With near virtuoso fingerpicking, the boy riffs on his dad's singing and strumming of an acoustic guitar. The dad exclaims:

—¡Feliz aniversario, centro comercial! ¡Treinta y cuatro años!

Another tray with tiny cups of sweet wine goes around. Some grab one and drink. A woman across from me sits in the circle of chairs with a wool blanket over her legs, listening to the music. I notice a few children playing with balloons inside the circle. Otherwise, it is the afternoon lull. Women with sleeping babies in their arms snooze themselves. The band's cheerful, upbeat music fills up what is now a waiting dance floor.

> No quiero que me hagas recordar
> Hoy quiero tomar para olvidar

Drinking to forget heartbreak or misfortune is a stereotypical huayno theme. A few people walk across the dance floor on unrelated business, taking a shortcut to somewhere. They don't carry shopping bags, just purses, backpacks, or a jacket folded over an arm. Through a gap in the blue nylon tarp, I see a strip of leaden sky. It is near dusk. A group of middle-aged men and women eventually gets up to dance. They grab hands and gyrate counterclockwise. Two steps forward, one backward, two forward again, everyone in sync. They laugh and wave at others to come to the floor. Minutes later, the dancing circle takes up half the courtyard.

Señor Condori keeps an eye on the unfolding scene like an entitled but anxious host looking for reassurance that his guests are having fun. He chats with Señor Martín, a current member of the Education Committee. I met Martín a few days ago in this very courtyard at an event he organized. It was a motivational talk by a lawyer and former radio personality about Peruvians' unique brand of entrepreneurialism. I knew the speaker. We overlapped a year or two in college, when he was an active left-wing student leader. He later had a political about-face and became a libertarian and admirer of Ayn Rand. The speaker not only renounced his leftist politics but did so to join the ranks of entrepreneurs and promoters of "popular capitalism." A radical rejoinder to marginality theory that is even further to the right of de Soto, popular capitalism foregrounds individual responsibility and advocates for zero regulations and total freedom and autonomy for doing business. The state is a blood-sucking ogre looking to kill all ingenuity and creativity. When the speaker later entered politics, he joined Castañeda Lossio's party and then switched to Fuerza Popular, the party of Keiko Fujimori.

At the event, the speaker began with a rhetorical question:

—What is the education of successful entrepreneurs? A master's degree? No! The street!

He didn't say that besides being a lawyer, he had an MBA degree from a reputed school.

My notes of his address that day are full of down-with-the-people, vernacular expressions that, it seems to me, aimed to offset his middle-class habitus and connect with his largely male, working-class and working-poor audience. He also prodded them with crass homophobic remarks. He told late arrivals who were filing into rows of chairs that were already pretty full, "No faggotry, okay? No pinching each other!" People in the audience chuckled and stirred with embarrassment. It instantly positioned him as the real macho in the room. The rest of the talk, the speaker availed himself of a strawman, an "unga, galunga, unga"–uttering primitive man who, unlike hardworking, rational individuals, trusts in a witch doctor to tell him what to do.

I couldn't believe what I was hearing. I can't believe it now going through my notes. I even wrote down a preposterous fictional anecdote about a man who invents a spear and hunts more wild pigs than others. He is envied because of his riches until he gets "three wives and becomes poor." The audience laughed. His overall point was that good entrepreneurs are ingenious and disciplined; they avoid overdependence at all costs, including letting the feelings or opinions of others guide their actions. It is all from Rand's playbook but trivialized and dumbed down, a pep talk about individualism and self-reliance given at the expense of "faggots" and women in the form of gluttonous, do-nothing "wives."

Like they do now at the anniversary party, Condori and Martín stood in the back, keeping an eye on the event. At the end of my notes are remarks that, I see now, were always going to be the endpoint message of the speaker to the vendors: It is imperative to accept change. In the provinces outside of Lima, vendors like them are already building malls! One must change when one is succeeding, not when one is struggling. It is not just a probuilding message but a message to build *now*. The speaker also promotes his own business and himself as an advisor. He tells vendors he can help them become direct importers, avoiding intermediaries, by facilitating their attendance to an upcoming import-export megafair in Canton, China. Judging by the muted response, his offer landed flat, perhaps an overwhelming, out-of-reach proposition for vendors.

28

Bataille's "Formless" was written for a "critical dictionary" that, he explained, "would start from the moments in which it no longer provides the meaning of their words but their job." More than on the meaning of *formless*, then, Bataille compelled us to focus on what the word *does* when uttered. Formless, for Bataille, issues from a well of affective potential and is spoken in reaction to a feeling of disgust and with the aim to debase. To call something formless is to defile it, to say it is deformed and deforming, and to link it to things that we fear and despise—"a spider or spit"—for the challenge they present to our language, structures, and systems.

Fred Botting and Scott Wilson argue that to call something formless is not to say that it lacks form. It is to summon forth an excess that our structures and systems themselves produce and suppress as they impose order in the world, and it is to affirm it as capable of ruining those structures and systems from within their limits. Formless testifies to what exceeds regulative forms, exploding sense and system, Botting and Wilson write, through an "intense and incomplete movement within and away from governing structures."

Many social science scholars in Peru interpret poorly regulated vending, building, and manufacturing in exactly the opposite terms. In their accounts, these activities exert pressure from without, expressing a demand for inclusion from the margins of formal society when it is unable or unwilling to expand access to the circuits of the modern economy. The idea that skirting regulations signals a desire for inclusion—Eliana Chávez called it a "modality of insertion" into the system—was for a long time an unquestioned assumption. In an early rendering of this idea, de Soto wrote:

> The greatest hostility immigrants met [in Lima] was from the legal system. . . . It was extremely difficult for them to formally access housing or an education and, above all, enter business or find a job. . . . Immigrants discovered that . . . the system was not willing to accept them, that barriers multiplied, that they had to wrest every right from an unwilling *status quo*, that they were on the margins of the convenience and benefits of the law.

This is how, de Soto concludes, *el Perú profundo* began its "long and sustained battle to integrate itself into formal life."

But understanding poor abidance of regulation as a system failure assumes confidence in the Peruvian state as a rationalizing entity and its bureaucracy as capable of incorporating every economic initiative into its systems. It assumes, in other words, an idealized and narrow vision of the economy that emphasizes rationality, productivity, order, and a teleology of progress to the exclusion of forms of social and economic behavior not wholly governed by these principles. Against this narrow perspective, Bataille's focus on potlatch economies redirects our attention to the forces that defy productivity, order, and bureaucratic forms and that produce value that must be lost or sacrificed despite attempts to regulate or repress it. These excesses encompass the formless, which includes intransigent base materiality—think of El

Hueco's hole and squalid building. This repulses and offends because it is "foreign to ideal human aspirations" such as reason, order, and architectural form as superior values and refuses "to be reduced to the great ontological machines resulting from those aspirations."

Bataille's formless explodes the formal-informal binary like an irritating, abominable third term. Neither Weber's formal rationality (of abstract laws and bureaucracies) nor the purported absence of that rationality, formless, like potlatch, thrives by pushing reasonableness beyond its limits and warping sense and system from the inside. El Hueco and Mesa Redonda warp the historical, political, economic, and patrimonial significance of downtown Lima. Cloaked in an aura of provocation, they flout UNESCO's designation and the World Monuments Fund's list of the one hundred most threatened heritage sites in the globe, which includes the historic center. The unsentimental, practical use of space does not just scoff at Lima's heritage; it keeps it on the brink of obliteration. And yet, if the markets produce a feeling of repulsion, they also generate enormous attraction.

The transgressions associated with these extreme spaces, as Sánchez Rodríguez might call them, and the bodies and objects that inhabit them generate a pull toward them for the vitality, pleasure, and excitement they promise regardless, or maybe because, of the way they threaten pollution, destruction, and death. Drawing on Bataille's ideas about architecture and its power to attract and to repel, Hollier explains that, for Bataille, certain social spaces that result from this power become points where "attraction-repulsion as a pair break down" and where repulsion becomes attractive and attraction repulsive. I see El Hueco and Mesa Redonda, precisely, as two such points.

They are centerpieces to a landscape shaped by forces that now push toward Weberian form and now toward Bataillean formlessness, coalescing and colliding in a frenzy of mimesis and contagion that engenders social and material realities inassimilable to one another. We can call this the formless in bureaucratic forms. This acts on the world by defiling it but also by opening up the possibility of delving into the multiplicities of vendors' economic lives, as Roitman would have it: by being receptive to the manifold dimensions of their experience and to the way their social worlds are fashioned by the law and the transgression of the law, the logic of gifts and countergifts, human rationality and a love of excess, the capricious will of gods and spirits, the array of human emotion from affection and solidarity to envy and resentment, and, importantly, by events toward which we have limited control, such as earthquakes, fires, and curses.

29

The number of dancers on the floor ebbs and flows. I go back up to the balcony to see the boy play from up close. He is the star of the show, and he knows it. His skill is remarkable, and many in the audience, including me, listen riveted. Behind me, the cooks in all but one of the kitchen concessions are almost done cleaning up. Their large empty pots have been put upside down to dry. The chairs in the dining area are also upside down on top of the tables, and two men go around mopping the floor. The food court is nearly empty. The only bustle interfering with the music is past the bathrooms, near a side entrance, on the sidewalk, where workers wave menus and also rubber soles at passersby to lure them to their food and shoe-repair stands.

It is an incongruent convergence of worlds: the boy's awe-inducing solos, the dancing, the anxious jostling outside, and a little beyond, across Abancay, the stern Courts tower attending to state business. Do these worlds ever touch? I imagine the courts' staff sometimes walk across the avenue for lunch and some shopping at El Hueco. It is certain vendors occasionally have to go across in the other direction to take care of official matters. Then, there is the great equalizer every October with the Lord of Miracles citywide procession. The intersection between building and hole is a regular stop on the procession's route, and when the Lord does stop there, a centuries-old history and a complicated present flatten into the pressing moment of the now.

In 1914 José Carlos Mariátegui, founder of Peru's Socialist Party, wrote a chronicle of the procession. Mariátegui appreciated the aesthetic, mystical, and political dimensions of the fervor of masses of devotees, led by Afro-Peruvians from the working-class barrios of Lima, moving through the city's narrow streets and swaying in unison. Feeling himself vulnerable to it, he noted that, despite its humble origins, the procession's power of attraction was so strong that even "the most aristocratic and elegant ladies" joined in. Dominant, seductive, oppressive, and irresistible, adjectives used by Mariátegui to convey the authority wielded by the Lord's image, the procession, which kept growing in size after the seventeenth century, fused the bodies and willpowers of *limeños* and *limeñas*, noble and plebeian alike, into a kind of social consensus incarnate in the mystically enraptured crowd. Year after year, Mariátegui wrote, the procession followed the same two-day itinerary. It covered the entire "old city," avoiding the "suburbs,"

parts of Lima that today are inside downtown. "In the punctuality and fixity of that route one feels the intense heartbeat of tradition. Nothing modifies them. Nothing upsets them." The devotees knew where the Lord could be found at any hour of the day.

Over the last century, however, the route did change, and the procession was extended to five days. It is now more massive than ever. Hundreds of thousands, decked in all hues of purple and immersed in a cloud of incense, move like an ocean tide to the languid cadence of the tunes played by several brass bands. From the 1920s to the 1960s, governments and the church, in a populist move, increasingly embraced the Lord of Miracles for political purposes, with mandataries and archbishops openly paying him tribute in Lima's main plaza. Estranged during the 1970s military dictatorship, there was rapprochement between government and cult in the 1980s under Alan García that intensified during the Fujimori years because of the ascendance as archbishop of ultraconservative Cardinal Juan Cipriani, who relied on the Lord of Miracles to try to stop the bleeding of parishioners to the ranks of Pentecostalist and other Protestant churches.

Today, the procession covers a large area of the city in routes that vary year by year to visit not just the former "suburbs" but also sites outside the limits of El Cercado, including the district of La Victoria. The Lord visits sites both of undisputed religious and political power, such as Lima's cathedral and archbishopric, the presidential and municipal palaces, the congress building, the Constitutional Tribunal, the national and central reserve banks, and the Palace of Justice. But that is not all. Along the way, he stops to be honored by the central command of the armed forces and the national police as well as by senior staff at the Ministry of Economics and at public hospitals. His route also includes sojourns to private establishments, like Club de la Unión, and commercial ones, like Importaciones Hiraoka and the supermarket chain Metro, retail powerhouses in Lima whose political clout equals their economic influence.

Mariátegui and Rostworowski both grapple with the Lord of Miracles's surreptitious powers of transformation and with his abilities to reassemble hierarchies and elevate plebeian hybridity to the highest spheres of Catholic sovereignty, compelling the most vaunted institutions of the nation, the military and the police, to bow to him. El Hueco is not listed as a stop in the Lord's official trajectory published every year, but on at least four occasions the maps show him passing in front of the market's main entrance. The vendors' newsletter of 2009 states that the procession made a twenty-minute stop "to bless all the faithful, devotees, and vendors of our commercial center." Vendors met the Lord with flowers and gifts and a twenty-four-square-meter carpet made of flower petals while a band played creole music in his honor. The 2014 newsletter also says that vendors were "lucky to have the Sacred Image of the Lord of Miracles of the Church of Las Nazarenas visit" them the previous October. This "obviously thrilled vendors, who did their utmost to welcome and pay homage to the Lord of Pachacamillas." The official map that year has, indeed, the heavy anda passing again in front of El Hueco's entrance.

When the world-famous Lord of Miracles stops by a hub of piracy, contraband, and forged goods, the magnitude of its political power flashes into view. The clarity of this moment is only partial and fleeting as the highest of the high and the lowest of the low briefly come into contact to reveal their secretive alliance. In a choreographed meeting of opposites, Lima's maximum Lord stoops down to bless El Hueco and, I surmise, also its sabotage of urban planning as a statecraft tool. The connection between El Hueco and the Lord is there for all to see, openly performed in the most public of public feasts. And, as Michel Taussig might argue, the mystery of how this complicity works is fortified in its revelation: How low into the hole and how high into the realm of political power goes the Lord's influence to embolden the defiant vendors of El Hueco might never be for us to know.

30

A group of dancers walks into the market. They wear black and red sweatpants and zip-up jackets. The women have ribbon-laced braids, and one wears an Indigenous bowler hat. In the twilight, a white florescent glow now pours out onto the courtyard. One electronics stand has seven TVs on display, all on the same channel. The dance floor is empty again, and one last round of plates of cabrito arrives to feed the latecomers.

A music recording with recognizable Amazonian sounds comes onto the speakers. Four couples spring onto the dance floor. The women wear ruffled shirts and wraparound miniskirts of printed Shipibo-Conibo motifs. The men wear long, baggy tunics with similar print patterns. All wear woven headbands and dance barefoot. The dancers leap and twirl in the open space to the beat of the music. Minutes later, they have been replaced by another group of four, these dancers decked out in black pants and red button-down shirts (the men) and flowing red skirts and one-shoulder, waist-tie tops (the women) for a coastal, Afro-Peruvian *festejo*. Whereas the Amazonian dance was all hops and twirls, the festejo is all hip and shoulder motions. Finally, the last set is predictably an Andean huayno dance, predictably because the show unfolds along the old, trodden folklore trope of representing Peru's three natural regions, coast, sierra, and jungle. The men wear pants, shirts, and ponchos pulled over their shoulders; the women wear puff skirts, shoulder wraps, and bowler hats. Everyone applauds after each dance, which, in spite of their hackneyed content, are well-rehearsed and executed performances. No donors are listed for this show. I assume it is at the administration's expense.

The dancers leave the circle, and night falls quickly after that. A crate of beer is now near the chairs and is missing a few bottles. The evening party has begun. I see the dance troupe, back in their sweatpants and zip-ups, file out of the market. I see Olvido alongside two other women leave too.

❉

IV

Evening and Next Morning

31

Off to one side of the courtyard, Señor Condori has sat down with others and broken off the main circle. An open bottle of beer is going around, paired with a small glass. One of the men fills up the glass, passes the bottle to his neighbor, and drinks. He shakes the glass upside down—maybe just to empty it, maybe to share its contents with pacha, the earth—and passes the glass to the next man. Condori calls me over.

—Did you eat?

I say I had plenty to eat and thank him for the delicious food.

—Come back tomorrow, yes? We have more to talk about. Come early, before it gets busy. Ten is good. Do you know where the main office is?

I very well know where the main office is. I have known since one of the first times I walked into El Hueco. César Miranda and I were at the end of a field outing. He had taken off his official caution-yellow vest, and we had given in to the temptations that Mesa Redonda throws at you at every turn, ogling the stands for good deals, as he and I were prone to do. At the corner of Jirón Ayacucho and Nicolás de Piérola, Miranda suggested we step into El Hueco. I followed him down the ramp toward the far back corridors. He wanted to take a quick look at a contention wall that abuts the neighbor's property. The neighbor had claimed it was caving in and took the cooperative to court. It was one of the multiple challenges vendors at El Hueco were facing with regards to the status of their property—both its legitimate ownership and the degree of safety for occupancy. The area nearest to the contention wall looked like a construction site.

—What a mess—Miranda muttered to himself.

Back on top of the ramp, private security guards, buff men in uniforms sporting El Hueco's logo, ambled about an ATM booth with Global Net services and watched over the stairwell that leads to the president's office. If El Hueco was anything like the newspapers said, the international banking booth and uniformed guards lent it a patina of uprightness. It struck me as a clever play of surface and depth with something still enigmatic about the market possibly lying beneath the smooth, orderly veneer.

Miranda hopped up the stairs to the president's office with an attitude both of familiarity and authority. At the end of the hallway, Roberto's assistant sat at her desk. She saw Miranda approach and reacted instinctively.

—He's busy.

—No problem. We'll wait.

Miranda spoke casually. He plopped on one of three empty chairs set up against the wall. I sat next to him. Seeing that we were prepared to wait as long as it was necessary, the assistant got up from her desk and walked over to Roberto's office.

—Give me a minute.

Miranda whispered to me with a sly smile:

—He's not busy.

Sure enough. The assistant came right back out, looking unhappy, followed by Roberto himself.

Miranda was trusted by street and market vendors but also feared; he was friendly and patient but never oblivious to the power he wielded. My impression, then and now, is that he genuinely thought businesses were better off obtaining a license, and so he didn't mind bending backward when needed to facilitate the process. He much preferred that over punishing. But when Miranda stepped out of his office on Jirón Camaná and walked over to Abancay wearing his official vest, countless looks would furtively turn away to avoid direct eye contact with him. Sometimes, a slight, nearly imperceptible stiffening of limbs betrayed the sudden discomfort his presence generated in this area of the city.

Roberto looked concerned and greeted us seriously but politely. Like elsewhere, it was a sign of El Hueco's state of legal insecurity that dread would descend on the market the second Miranda's unannounced arrival was noticed. Then, his interactions with vendors required gallons of grease to ease the grating tensions that emerged between his relatively simple goals and the complicated reality of the markets. On the one hand, there was Miranda's overhaul of the legislation to make it friendlier to campos feriales, not as they could be in some vague future but as they were now, in and around the historic center. On the other hand, there were the extant rifts among vendors, their deep ambivalence, and their ever wavering will to meet even the most minimum requirements for legalization. Few markets were in a position to turn down Miranda's offer to help out. Most had to at least play along.

We sat in front of Roberto's desk. Miranda started:

—We're just passing by and wanted to say hello, check how things are going. We saw the wall is going up very nicely.

Grease.

—Yes, we're almost done with it.

Roberto seemed to relax. His shoulders loosened, and he reclined on his chair. Miranda introduced me as a student of anthropology, and Roberto handed me a promotional calendar. On it was the same digital rendering of a modern building, all glass and steel, that was on the billboard over the market's courtyard. They weren't anywhere close to breaking ground, and Miranda knew it, but Roberto said this is what El Hueco would soon look like. With Miranda's help, it will be a multistory mall like the one in the picture. More grease.

As we walked out of the market, Miranda said to me that Arispe is good.

—I give him a hard time, but he's a good one. Honest, smart. He gets it. He tries and tries against the odds. He's been here from the beginning. He'll tell you everything you need to know.

Miranda was right about Roberto.

32

Señor Condori doesn't invite me to join his group. They are all men. They are drinking and laughing. I sit in an empty chair in the main circle. The lighting in the courtyard has dimmed. I notice it is because the nearby stands have rolled down their doors. More chairs break off the circle, and more beer bottles circulate. I look around but don't see Roberto anywhere.

On the balcony, a man grabs the mic and announces the first dancing band of the night:

—¡Los engreídos olímpicos de Huancayo!

The Pampered Olympians of Huancayo. The announcer goes on:

—Drawn by the affection and friendship of the people of El Hueco,
they have come to offer their music to us.

The singer of the band wears a black button-down shirt and a gold
and silver vest embroidered with hummingbirds. He steps in front
of the band while the wind instruments begin with a slow tune. It is
a *muliza*. Its rhythm imitates the pace of walking mules. It used to
be favored by muleteers of the central Andes, where Huancayo is,
and it is typically played as a party opener. The singer calls out to
his paisanos:

—Where are the people from Jauja? Tarma? Junín?

Then, he begins to sing:

> Cuando estés con él, dile
> Cuando estés con él, cuéntale
> Dile que anoche estuviste conmigo
> Dile, dile que anoche estuviste conmigo
> ¡Dile!

The miserable pleadings of a paramour to his lover to tell her hus-
band she was with him last night, to tell him the story of them, flow
down to the dance floor, where people move to the unhurried beat,
holding hands in twos or threes and taking turns passing beer bottle
and glass. The muliza's tempo speeds up a little, and the lyrics change
in theme if not in mood.

> La orquesta que me va a acompañar
> cuando yo muera
> Ya está contratada, cancelada
> Y bien pagada

They turn to the self-pitying words of a man who has himself hired
and paid in full the musical band that will accompany his funeral.
Scorned, he goes on to ask his lover not to attend or pretend to cry
because she has never really loved him. The song is slow and sad but
somehow also intensely rousing. The atmosphere on the dance floor
simmers to the point of exuberance.

—Three hurrahs for Centro Comercial El Hueco! And one! And two! And three!

The singer hollers as the band switches to a fast-paced and extremely danceable *huaylas*, a central Andes form of huayno.

Sácame la vuelta
¡Pero no me dejes!

"Cheat on me. But don't leave me!" the singer's voice resounds across the courtyard. The dance floor is now packed. Señor Martín and some of the other elders lightly stamp their feet to the music's rhythm. But the vast majority of the crowd are young people. About half of them dance in couples, man and woman. The other half stands and watches. Women's presence is sparer among those standing. The young women with babies are gone. The dancing pairs swing around each other. They come close but do not touch. Their bodies barely graze one another before they twirl away to switch places. They laugh. A man in front of me leans his upper body forward and lifts his arms, swaying them in the air over his dancing partner's shoulders. She leans back slightly, away from him, and throws him a broad and flirty smile. Their bodies come close again in a move filled with the subtle tension of seduction, and then spin away. It is a well-known huaylas, and the two of them are blissfully singing along.

The ceremonial demands of earlier in the day are over. There is nothing left to do but kick back, enjoy the music, dance, play, and let go. The MC is on the dance floor, his jacket and tie are off, his shirt's neck button undone. I don't feel unwelcome to stay, maybe the opposite. At this stage of the celebration there is an intimate feel, a relaxed vibe that invites one to give up all concerns. A bottle comes around my way. I don't drink when I am in the field, but I know better than to turn it down. I pour just enough to wet my lips and give pacha a small drink, and pass bottle and glass along. But the warm, sensual intimacy that permeates the courtyard is precisely what makes me hesitate. My studious gaze abruptly feels meddlesome, self-serving, prying, out of place.

I feel I should leave. In my head I want to stay, but in my body I want to go. Or is it the other way around? I hear the roar of the evening's rush hour traffic outside. It is the end of the workday and the shopping trip downtown. A taxi line has formed, many old and decrepit and part of the legion of nonregulated cabs that roam the city. They have a bad reputation. Harrowing stories regularly do the rounds in Lima as does advice for women for how to detect red flags before getting in. How late is it safe to stay? How much should people drink before it is unacceptable for me to observe or talk to them? I think to myself, I am invited and do not want to miss the rest of the biggest party of the year at El Hueco. But my legs take me away from the courtyard, and before I know it I am outside standing on the sidewalk.

The landscape has totally morphed. There is a luminescence that comes from the reflection of headlights in the foggy air. The avenue and sidewalk, already with a film of pooled mist on their surface, mirror the traffic and lamppost lights in bright, blurry smudges. It makes the grimy city center look beautiful, magical. People gather in corners and on curbs to wait for their microbus. At this hour the vehicles are bursting. They honk their horns and drown the street hawkers' calls. Some arrive too full and barely slow down to spit out a passenger or two before speeding back up. Those left behind wait patiently for the next one.

I walk to Estación La Colmena, where I take the Metropolitano bus, line B, to close to the end of the route. The bus is also packed, suffocatingly so, and at every stop more people ram in. When the bus is this way, I have to find a surface on which to lean back and put my backpack as a buffer in front of me. Then, it is all about enduring the hot, sweaty, uncomfortable ride.

When I began going to El Hueco and Mesa Redonda for research, the Metropolitano system didn't exist. There were only two forms of semipublic transportation to travel from Lima's southern districts to the center: a slew of microbuses that rode along the entire length of access roads of the Vía Expresa, stopping at innumerable lights and taking an hour and a half in the thickest traffic to traverse the meager seven miles of distance; and the infamous *colectivos*, sedan cars that collected passengers and took the Vía Expresa to Plaza Grau. The freeway was always congested, as it is still today, but the grubby colectivos still cut the travel time in half.

The Metropolitano was inaugurated in 2010. It had a rocky start as it was at first more expensive and unable to compete with the microbuses along the same route. Up until then, the entire public transportation system in Lima functioned through route concessions. A person or association obtained a license for a route from the municipal government,

tapped private owners of buses or microbuses, usually rebuilt old vehicles to run the route, and hired drivers and *cobradores,* money collectors, to operate the vehicles on said route. It was one of those regimes of exception put in place to have minimal control over a nonregulated service. Most of Lima's public transportation operates this way even today—an iteration of the formless in bureaucratic forms—favoring private interests recalcitrant to change and shortchanging the public with terrible service.

Polvos Azules zips by as the Metropolitano leaves the district of La Victoria behind. The original Polvos Azules predated El Hueco. It was one of the oldest campos feriales in downtown Lima, named after the street block where it was located, which in colonial times was the site of a tannery that dyed cow hides with indigo powders. It sat along the Río Rímac behind the Presidential Palace. In the 1980s and early 1990s, people went there from all over the city to buy pirate and contraband goods during a time when imports were banned. Then the market burned down in 1993. The cause of the fire, as is typical of these disasters, was never determined. Some say it was triggered by an appliance connected to an improvised cable. Others say that it was sabotage. Twenty-five hundred vendors lost everything, but no one died. I remember when it happened. The horrors of the fire spread by word of mouth because a Shining Path bombing of electric towers along the

Carretera Central had left the city without power that morning. Polvos Azules relocated to the concrete mall along the Vía Expresa we just passed on the bus. From the Metropolitano, you can't miss it. The entire boxy structure is painted in bright powder blue.

I make it home at about 11 p.m., when the last band of the day, Orquesta Latin Boom, is slated to play at El Hueco. I sit at a table in my room to type up my notes and download from my phone around two hundred photos. These include the Beneficencia's archive documents. I collate and begin to read them more closely. The history of El Hueco's property is a puzzle. As I go through the documents, my questions grow in number.

33

Sometime after 1941 a sliver of the Santa Teresa convent went to broaden Abancay, and a sliver of Santa Rosa de Candamo's hospice went to expand Nicolás de Piérola. What happened with the rest of the property? With the colonial buildings demolished, what did the land look like during the decade before the construction of the state buildings began? That decade spans the last years of World War II through part of Odría's Ochenio. It is baffling that neither the second tower nor anything else went up in the corner lot because this was a period of rapid urban modernization and expansion, and Odría was a builder president, a public works kingpin who built up a storm in Lima.

Ownership of the Santa Teresa property was often unclear and disputed over the nearly two hundred years after the Carmelite nuns were pushed out of their convent. The seized building first housed a school for orphan girls. Presbyter Don Francisco Navarrete served as director of the school and chaplain of the Church of Santa Teresa for thirty years. The Beneficencia was created in 1834, but it isn't until the presbyter's death in 1859 that it enters into possession of everything: school, church, and the whole of the Santa Teresa estate. More than half a century later, in 1924, the Beneficencia carries out an appraisal of the property but, inexplicably, excludes the church area. It took two consecutive sets of laws, in 1935 and 1939, for the Beneficencia to secure—to formalize or regularize—its property rights and full dominion over the old convent,

Un hermoso claustro de Santa Terera

church, and hospice. The laws were retroactive dictums affirming the institution's rights over all inherited, donated, or adjudicated assets in its de facto possession.

Despite these blanket laws, in 1941 the Beneficencia's director demands an inquiry and a proclamation on the charitable institution's rights over the property given that the buildings will "in brief be demolished for the opening of an avenue." The head of the legal office issues a report detailing how the Beneficencia came to own convent and hospice; he writes that after reviewing both documents and legislation, there is no doubt the institution is the sole owner of Santa Teresa and all its assets. It is less conclusive about the hospice for "lack of evidence." The Beneficencia, the report states, can thus give any part of the Santa Teresa land over to the provincial council of Lima for their planned expansion in exchange for fair compensation. Indeed, a payment in money and trade-in properties owned by the city was made in 1948 for part of the property, which a 1959 document refers to as a "sale."

I am decidedly deep down the rabbit hole. I am enthralled by all those details, and they pull me in with the possibility that they might amount to a straightforward, fact-based story. But what kind of facts am I looking for? Isn't the obvious absence of certain kinds of information also evidence to weigh in? What answer to the puzzle of the abandoned hole can the archive supply that will appease my curiosity, settle my doubts, or at least tell a sufficiently satisfying story? I don't know. But I keep going.

The avenues broadened and elongated, and the Ministry of Education tower finished, the documents at the archive turn to the remaining piece of land, now a forsaken foundation pit. A 1957 letter from the Ministry of Hacienda and Commerce requests information from the Beneficencia about the value of the leftover property and expresses interest in acquiring it. Days later, an internal memo at the institution orders another appraisal with an eye to the sale. But there was no sale because two years later, the Beneficencia's president writes the letter to the minister of hacienda claiming that, since 1953, the property had been "occupied" by the central government without mediation of a legal process, either a sale or expropriation.

In 1959 the city's demographic explosion was in full swing, its population more than doubling between 1940 and 1961. In these two decades, which include the Ochenio, Lima's growth was most visible downtown, where the housing supply fell dismally short of the pace of demand. The documents from this period show an awareness of the increasing value of the former convent as real estate. In the 1959 letter by the Beneficencia's president, and in the exchange with the Hacienda and Commerce Ministry that ensued, the writers refer to the property as "valuable," noting the loss it has meant for the Beneficencia to have it idle in the hands of the central government. It also notes that the excavations and other unfinished works done in preparation for the canceled building have contributed to its depreciation. At one point, in a tone that suggests exasperation, the president of the Beneficencia asserts that he is moving to take back the property. Seven years later, architect Bryce's memo proposing a commercial building for the spot makes it clear that nothing has yet been built on it despite its "high commercial value."

After the 1978 letter from Lima's mayor to the president of the Beneficencia describing the foundation pit as a "public latrine" and advising that a tenant plans to temporarily build on the strip that is on street level, the archive goes quiet. At least in the files I was handed, there were no documents from the 1980s. The only one from the 1990s is the memo from 1997 that refers to the property as "the so-called Hueco de Abancay." The memo rehashes the entire history of ownership and details the area in square meters that was sold to COOPSE in 1989. It says that the sale was recorded "preventatively" in the public registers. I don't know what that means, but from a 1998 court ruling (not at the archive), I have learned that the year after the vendors were removed from the streets around Mercado Central, the Beneficencia sued COOPSE, asking for an injunction for it to stop "demolishing walls and erecting buildings in its property." The judge adjudicates in the Beneficencia's favor because the property title was still in its name.

It looks like the perennially ambiguous status of the property had incited bogus claims of ownership in the hopes of scoring a piece of it, such as the suit brought on by the heirs of some Señor Lorenzo Espejo Bravo, which a 2001 memo says "lacks foundation." But that same year, through a supreme decree, the sale to COOPSE is confirmed, and a new sale, of two thousand square meters the Beneficencia still owned, approved. The decree states that these sales are an "exceptional and extraordinary measure" and spells out an obligation by COOPSE to build a solid structure with commercial units for the cooperative's members within six years. That window of time, of course, has long been shut. I know from my conversations with Roberto that the fight in the courts for the rights to the hole did not really cease until 2007, when vendors were at last given full ownership.

34

Marxism is often called "historical materialism" for its focus on the material conditions of production as these evolve in history. Bataille's emphasis on consumption rather than production, and in particular on nonproductive consumption, is the basis for what he called *base* materialism. This includes sacrificial destruction and everything else that is inassimilable to productive systems because of its abjection— "all that is offensive, indestructible, and even despicable," in Bataille's words, "all that overthrows, perverts, and ridicules." A base-materialist reading of Marxism centers on the lumpenproletariat.

On the one hand, Bataille's critique of the bourgeoisie, whose hatred of expenditure he blames for the repression and near disappearance of potlatch-like economies, lines up with Weber's recounting of the emergence and consolidation of modern capitalism. Infused with the Protestant ethic that prizes work, accumulation, and a spare life, a capitalist rationality, according to Weber, is averse to more than minimal risk and is keen on efficiency, balanced accounts, and growth. Bataille argued that when the bourgeoisie does engage in expenditure, it is only to "squirrel away" its effects and destroy its brilliance. But on the other hand, Bataille also knew that capitalism exceeds the enterprising bourgeoisie. Capitalism, he wrote, "still harbors some traces of the glorious acts of earlier social formations." Few great, luxurious monuments are built these days that cannot be exploited for commercial gain, like the old Christian cathedrals were, but we can all observe the extravagances of financial speculation, in which enormous fortunes are put at stake and often lost, draining a society's surpluses. Bourgeois possessiveness and "gambler speculation" coexist in capitalism in a complementary way, Bataille noted, which led him to suggest that the class struggle would thus be not to overturn the ownership of the means of production, as in Marxism, but the ownership of the means of consumption.

It was the unique threat that the lumpenproletariat posed to capitalist rationality and class structure that inspired some of Marx's and Engels's contemporaries and later theorists to identify it as the true revolutionary subject. If Marx and Engels failed to abolish all nonproductive, base elements from the proletariat, Mikhail Bakunin, Bataille, and Frantz Fanon, among others, seized on this failure. As bourgeois individualism established itself as the norm globally, in an aspirational way even for the proletariat, it was imperative to reimagine the engine of revolutionary change by turning to the agonistic and antisocial efforts of the lowest classes of people, "those who push the consequences of current rationalist conceptions as far as they will go." Only a class struggle led by those who stand nothing to gain with the upending of the status quo would be able to challenge the existence of the bourgeoisie through "the grandest form of social expenditure."

For Bakunin, the fact that the lumpenproletariat was not driven, strictly speaking, by class-based interests put it at the center of the revolution. Only the outcasts of society—the millions of uncultivated, disinherited, miserable, illiterate, "that 'rabble' almost unpolluted by bourgeois civilization," he wrote—could bring about such revolutionary change. Fanon, for his part, argued that the lumpen was the true revolutionary force in anticolonial movements in the African continent since it was the only sector of society that didn't stand to benefit either from colonialism or from independence. The lumpen, in Fanon's words, were like rats gnawing at the roots of a tree preparing to invade the colonialist city "by the most underground channels" to threaten its security like a "gangrene eating into the heart of colonial domination."

The idea of a class struggle spearheaded by those extruded from the class structure was an outrage to the idealism of bourgeois revolutionaries, said Bataille. It would also be an outrage later in the twentieth century when marginality theorists like Quijano and Nun reexamined Latin America's revolutionary prospects in light of the fast depeasantization and urban explosion underway in the region, resulting in the unprecedented growth of the non–wage-earning labor market. The sheer size and concentration in cities of this marginal mass, Nun said, fueled its capacity for organization and violence. But like Marx regarding the lumpenproletariat, Quijano and Nun remarked on the political fickleness of this social stratum and on the evidence of its easy cooptation to reactionary causes.

Quijano linked marginality to "*lo cholo*" and, again, to fickleness. No longer Indigenous and not quite urban or mestizo, lo cholo, for Quijano, moves "between various normative worlds" and finds "refuge in its marginal condition." In it, lo cholo wields an ample margin of freedom with behaviors typically deemed disrespectful of institutions and "scandalous" from both an Indigenous and an urban or creole point of view, and "the cholo mocks" the outrage this produces. As a trait of the *révolté*, lo cholo is innovative, a most active and entrepreneurial force of change in our society, Quijano argues. In what she terms "the cholo act," Urpi Montoya Uriarte points to the novel ways Andean and urban dress, language, and foods have been brought together, such as in the famous *combinado*, which combines on the same plate, side by side, ceviche and pasta. The combinado is a popular dish served in downtown streets and markets that upsets the way both foods are traditionally eaten in middle-class environments, where the combinado often provokes disgust.

Marginal mass or lumpen, a revolution with a protagonist occupying such an uneasy and volatile position outside the class and labor structure could never be the redemptive leap that would make a people rise above all other classes. It would rather have to emulate the dirty, subterranean work of an "old mole." The figure of an "old mole" as evocative of the revolutionary upsurge was Marx's own. Bataille reformulates it as the figure of a base-materialist revolution that would detonate "in the bowels of the earth, as in the materialist bowels of [lumpen] proletarians." Against the bankrupt and decrepit edifice of bourgeois culture and ethics, the old mole revolution would hollow out "chambers in a decomposed soil repugnant to the delicate nose of the [bourgeois] utopians." Indeed, a politics of the lumpen.

35

To beat the worst of the bus stampede during the morning rush hour, I leave to go back to El Hueco at 7 a.m. The sky is its usual leaden gray, but there is no precipitation. Downtown awakes as I leave Estación La Colmena. Storefronts keep their doors rolled up midway as an attendant sweeps the front sidewalk. Only breakfast carts offering *pan con*

palta, fresh-squeezed orange juice, and *emoliente*, a sweet, hot herbal drink, are open for business. Customers stand by to eat and drink. At El Hueco, a private security guard leans against the open door browsing on his phone. I know I am early, but I step inside anyway to confirm the office is closed. It is, but I don't mind. I take the opportunity to go by La Cochera in Mesa Redonda. The campo ferial has been the site of three fires in five years. The last one was two months ago.

The market sells auto parts and other hardware like power cords and lighting fixtures. Some of these are knockoffs. I recently heard on the radio that 15 percent of cabling sold in Lima is *bamba*, which broadly means "not the real thing," something of a shoddy, low quality. This presents a problem because the stands at La Cochera and other such markets require a good supply of electricity for their displays, and substandard wiring easily causes fires.

When Miranda was in office, the president of La Cochera at the time told him vendors wanted to apply for an operating license. Miranda was all in. The problem was that the vendors had opened an unauthorized passageway to the market directly behind La Cochera. This passageway linking the markets was, commercially speaking, a brilliant idea. Foot traffic swelled as they had effectively created a shortcut between two busy streets. But legally, it broke every rule in the book. The Office of Civil Defense demanded that the passageway either be shut or that the markets apply for a joint safety certificate, which was indispensable for a license. Both were consequential decisions that required a full roster of signatures from vendors in both markets. On a day we visited, Miranda and La Cochera's president were in a stalemate about the passageway. Miranda let himself into the president's office without knocking, with me trailing behind. There were startled looks. Two men sitting in front of the president's desk jumped to their feet. Regrouping, the president stretched a hand to greet Miranda and then offered us the chairs where his visitors had been sitting. The visitors stood to the side during our brief stay. The reason for Miranda's surprise visit was understood. He looked at the president in the eye and asked with a smirk:

—So?

—Hanging in there. Pérez says he's doing okay getting the signatures.

Pérez was a lawyer the vendors had hired. Miranda seemed pleased.

—Oh, fantastic! And how long do you think that will take?

—He'll have them all by next week. He's making good progress.

—Oh, wonderful! But push him along, no? Otherwise, you are going to be landed a hefty fine.

Miranda chuckled. His tone was lighthearted, but the scarcely veiled threat felt like a sting.

—No, pues, let's hope not!

The president looked disgruntled and blamed the vendors of the other galería as the ones dragging.

Soon, we were back outside, and now that the men were no longer within earshot, Miranda said to me:

—Bullshit. They're not going to do anything.

—Uh?

I thought the meeting had gone well. But it had all been grease in the grinding machinery. Grease, grease, grease.

In those days, La Cochera was a spectacle to behold. Hundreds of lamps and light bulbs of all sizes, shapes, and colors glowed inside the stands and corridors. Lime green, orange, red, and purple glass orbs glimmered. The corridors looked like the streets of a marvelous otherworld. But behind the phantasmagoria of lights, who knew how fragile or overloaded the electric grid running through the market was.

Then, in the summer of 2012, La Cochera burned down. When firefighters showed up, they found out that the market had no functioning fire hydrant nearby nor any other source of water. Vendors darted to the sturdier, slightly better prepared galería next door and begged to borrow their firefighting equipment. They were angrily turned away. But as the fire raged on and, through an open skylight, spread to several stands in their market, which sold stuffed animals, the neighbors had no choice but to tap their firefighting unit and help keep the flames at bay. The disaster was compounded, as is common, by the presence of looters. "They stole everything," said a vendor who evacuated La Cochera to a reporter. "Thieves took advantage of the desperate situation to plunder."

No one died that day, but almost half the stands in La Cochera and ten in the market next door were turned to ashes. News outlets pointed to an electric short circuit as the cause of the disaster but also to a gas cylinder that exploded. Additionally, there were rumors of a clandestine drug lab on the roof. As stories and tall tales went around, so did the admonitions and rebukes imparting blame, and this went on until the accounts devolved into the same murky picture that arises after every fire.

The ruins of La Cochera were still smoldering when the head of citizen security at the city government said that they had inspected La Cochera two months before. Finding that it lacked proper firefighting equipment and escape routes, it had ordered the market to shut down. But the vendors had obtained an injunction from a judge to keep it open. The next morning, Mayor Susana Villarán visited the premises and said no such injunction had been issued, and she accused city inspectors of neglect. Standing on a bed of scorched and wet debris, she explained that La Cochera had had an operating license issued in May 2010 by the previous city administration. That would have been during Miranda's time. Neither the cause of the fire nor who was responsible for letting La Cochera operate freely ever became clear. But vendors at poorly regulated markets like La Cochera do in fact often resort to injunctions as a dilation or obstruction tactic against closures. DESCO, one of Lima's most reputable NGOs, says in a report that injunctions are meant to protect vendor rights against undue losses in income while legal action is pending. But it explains that court measures like injunctions are at the heart of Lima's governance problems due to "bad judges" and the "Mafioso behavior of the local 'entrepreneurs' . . . who impose their own private interests over the needs of the city."

A video report on the day of the fire shows a young and terrified vendor crying. In between sobs, she describes cardboard boxes ablaze falling on her from the second story, where, she says, they had their storage spaces. Another vendor moans into the reporter's mic about his bank loan payments coming due.

—How am I going to pay them now?

The scene cuts to the raging fire as loud, intermittent explosions inside the market go pop, pop, pop. A municipal official, caution-yellow vest on, says with impassive resignation that those are overheated cans of paint. The reporter retorts:

—Highly flammable!

—Yes, it is a hardware and auto-parts market.

Once on Jirón Andahuaylas, just off the crooked Jirón de la Mesa Redonda, I pass by a branch of Interbank, one of the major banking institutions in Peru that, as the vendor in the video indicates, has a presence in the area because of their credit schemes. I then see the plain, black-and-white sign of La Cochera. The doors are open. I walk in and go all the way to the back. The passageway to the adjacent galería is still there, intact. As for the last fire of two months ago, I don't see any remaining signs of damage.

36

The rabbit hole of the archive yields a story about El Hueco's property that is only fragmentary. It offers no clear, fast answer to my question of why the hole was abandoned for nearly half a century. But if the gaps and opacities preclude a straightforward narrative, they also make room for unofficial tales and histories that can be inferred or extrapolated from them.

For example, the archival documents point to the broader reality of settler societies like Lima's, where the sinuous, haphazard path of regularization of El Hueco's property must surely have been the norm for land and landed estates before and since independence. For fifty years after Francisco Pizarro's arrival in the region, land was handed over to Spaniards, both in cities and the countryside, much as it happened with Pachacámac and Pachacamilla. A papal bull had extended to the "New World" the doctrine that "land won by conquest could be distributed by the conqueror." With the exception of land given directly by or on behalf of the king, as it was with the religious orders, property was generally bitterly contested, usually because of questions regarding the legitimacy of the granting authority. The new landowners' main interest, however, was the wealth to be extracted from their holdings, not securing property rights. But by the 1590s through the 1780s, Susan Ramírez reports that to correct tenure insecurity, assuage anxieties of expropriation, and encourage agricultural and other investment, several *visitas de la tierra*—land surveys—were sponsored by the Crown to "legalize" ownership of landholdings in the viceroyalty.

Around the time of Peru's independence in 1821, the nascent state's powers of eminent domain and a drastic turn to secularization in the new nation shook the foundations of titled property once more. In Lima, at least fourteen monasteries and convents were expropriated. Legal ownership of Santa Teresa's estate, as the archive shows, was in limbo for decades. For decades if not centuries, a common legal status for real estate in the city was one of undefinition and ongoing regularization, full of twists and turns. The budding bureaucracy was forced to deal with a situation that required it to adapt, bend its rules, or make one of exception to legalize what was already there ex post facto.

As the city entered the era of state-driven modernization, a new system of property rights certification via Registros Públicos was created in 1888. With the demolition of Lima's baroque wall and the building of the first modern boulevards following the wall's limits, property rights were affirmed not just by means of the public register but also of more eminent domain, court rulings, and laws, such as the ones from 1935 and 1939, which sought to put an end to uncertainties about possessions handed down from colonial times, such as many of the Beneficencia's properties. But it wasn't until 1994 through another institution created by Fujimori—the Superintendencia de Registros Públicos, or SUNARP—that various local and regional registers that had disparately coexisted for over a century merged into one. With respect to the Santa Rosa de Candamo hospice, for which documentation is rare, the 2001 report at the archives asserts it has been property of the Beneficencia since "time immemorial." It details that in 1965 the courts afforded the institution a "remedial" property title based on secondary documentation, such as meeting minutes and bulletins that prove the property has been under the Beneficencia's management since at least 1871 or "for a much longer time than 40 years," a textbook case of regularization.

From the 1940s through the end of the twentieth century, this state of legal fluidity of land exacerbated as the city's footprint grew at an exponential speed. De facto land occupation, followed by a medley of regularization strategies that culminated in COFOPRI, coalesced into a landscape that is permanently under (auto)construction. It is a patchwork of titled and untitled land, of legal and illegal buildings in all sorts of combinations where legal insecurity is too common. Amid all this, the twentieth century also saw a few waves of planned growth and consolidation. The first two were under dictatorial regimes: Augusto B. Leguia's eleven years in power, a period known as the Oncenio (1919–1930), when today's Avenidas Venezuela and Arequipa were built; and Odría's Ochenio. According to Dorota Biczel, Odría attempted to manage and discipline Lima's recent arrivals through built form. With Seoane's tower as a prime example of his style of central planning, he hoped that "transparency, luminosity, and hygiene would organize and order the ostensibly unruly, filthy migrant bodies and cohere them into a new and improved model social corpus." Odría, however, was also at the helm of the first efforts to accommodate immigrants as they moved into the young barrios around Lima and occupied sidewalks and roads with a flourishing street economy. De Soto asserts that Odría assisted leaders of land invasions in exchange for their political support, which lent him legitimacy. He understood their rising political clout and became an agent of what I have called the formless in bureaucratic forms.

In the 1960s, during President Belaúnde's first stint in office, Mayor Luis Bedoya Reyes built Lima's very first freeway, the Vía Expresa, along which the Metropolitano buses run today. Perhaps the most recent push in urban infrastructure expansion has been by Luis Castañeda Lossio during his three periods as mayor of Lima. Castañeda Lossio produced many works, as it is widely recognized today, and stole proportionally from the public coffers. He would leave office in 2018 in disgrace after incontrovertible evidence emerged of collusion, bribery, and money laundering in connection to the building projects he spearheaded.

Lima was founded eight miles away from the Pacific Ocean to protect it from pirates roaming those waters at the time. But ironically, there is a lot that strikes one as piratical in the way Lima has grown and consolidated itself as a city over the centuries. This piracy and its dreams of radical autonomy, as with the vendors of El Hueco and Mesa Redonda, paradoxically go hand in hand with dreams of regularization to obtain property titles and capitalize on the assets. This has been the main form of urbanization in Lima since what the archive calls "time immemorial."

37

I go across the illegal passageway to look around the galería in the back and exit on Jirón Paruro. I am a couple of blocks from Calle Capón, the heart of Lima's Barrio Chino, which abuts Mercado Central and Mesa Redonda. I can already see the thin, red columns and ornamental green tops of a Chinese portal, a *paifang* donated to the city in 1971 by Lima's Chinese community. Half a block past the portal is one of the main entrances to Mercado Central.

Since the 1997 eviction of street vendors from the surrounding streets, Mercado Central has come back to life. I don't know which came first: its recovery or Lima's gastronomic boom. They may be related because the market is a favorite shopping spot for the new crop of fancy chefs in the city. It being a food market, it is not just fully open and bustling at this time of the day; it is already past its peak hours. The sights and smells remind me of shopping with my mother as a young person at the markets of Surquillo and Magdalena. Resensitized since I moved abroad and shopping mainly at supermarkets, with their bloodless, cellophane-wrapped meat packages, the carcasses of animals—skinned, gutted, and splayed but identifiable as goatlings, piglets, guinea pigs, chickens, and pigeons—are a small shock to see. In these markets, they are often laid out on countertops or hung from hooks, as are cow and pig heads, legs, and ribs. The raw flesh, frozen grimaces, and lifeless stares as well as the abiding stench of blood and guts, strain only a little the air of normalcy that prevails around such signs of violence. The smell is both revolting and familiar. I imagine myself not just getting used to it but growing to like it again.

Today, I wonder how people can eat inside the market while engulfed in the stink of death. They do so with gusto, sitting at long counters between the mammals and the fish sections. I glance at their plates: ceviche, arroz con pollo, and cabrito and beans. Past the piles of corvina and striped tuna and the mounds of scallops and crab, with their corresponding stink, is the artisanal cheeses and grains sections. I am drawn to the towers of fresh cheese molds and accept tastes from the ones from Puno, Cuzco, and Arequipa. I buy a mold of the first, which has the perfect rubbery texture and level of salt and, I can swear, a whiff of the scent of the hands of the maker.

The Mercado's building is boxy and unremarkable. But it wasn't always like that. The site was the location of yet another fire of historical proportions. Lima has always wrestled with street vending. Traders, settled in public spaces, have been banned, tolerated, or otherwise accommodated by the city all through its history but never completely eradicated. In the 1850s, as was the trend in Europe, Marshall Ramón Castilla, Peru's three-time caudillo president, undertook the building of the first central market in a push to rein in the chaos and begin modernizing the city by replacing the old and insalubrious markets that had sprung up in Plaza Mayor and other neighborhood plazas and church atriums since before independence. Mercado de la Concepción, built on the site of the expropriated Monasterio de la Concepción,

Interior del Mercado de la Concepción, Lima. *4 octobre*
Edit. M. N. Benavides, Lima (Perú).

opened in 1905. It was designed in the fashionable Parisian-style of high vaulted ceilings but with a frame not of wrought iron but wood. Photos of the time show an elegant and delicate matchstick structure inside an adobe-brick perimeter wall. The building, however, was overrun by demand for space since its opening day.

One February morning in 1964, a gas stove exploded inside a stand. The decaying wood beams as well as the makeshift cardboard partitions that had been put in place for storage spaces fueled the fire, which consumed the building with unstoppable fury. Rumors spread that Mayor Bedoya Reyes had provoked the fire to finally get rid of the intractable, overcrowded market. He had attempted to evict the vendors by force and by means of police seizures and fines. But vendors kept coming back or their coveted spots would be instantly taken by other vendors. Bedoya Reyes replaced the market with today's functional, modernist building, which also became a magnet for street vendors, who gradually resettled around it, installing unauthorized connections to the city's electric grid and sewage system. These were the vendors who Mayor Andrade fought with special virulence until they agreed to relocate to El Hueco, Las Malvinas, and a location north of downtown.

With the mold of fresh cheese in my bag, I go out the market's side door and circle around to Jirón Ayacucho toward El Hueco. The door to Condori's office is now open. I go up the stairs. A copy of the calendar

Roberto gave me years ago with the digital rendering of the would-be building hangs from a cork board, its corners frayed and colors faded. The 2010 flip-book almanac that came with it is gone.

—I'm here to see Señor Condori.

Señorita Raquel, his assistant, tells me he is not in.

It is past 10 a.m., and it is a Friday. Few stands have opened, and there is hardly a shopper to be seen. The mood in the market is one of postparty slumber.

—Can I wait for him? He asked me to come by.

—Sure—she shrugs.

An hour later, I am restless. I tell Señorita Raquel I will be back and get up to leave. She shoots me a skeptical look. I go down to see if Roberto is in his stand.

With a loud belly laugh, Roberto informs me:

—He won't come!

He says the party ended at four this morning. Roberto seems to have himself pulled an overnighter. He is here because he has a delivery to make today. He sounds a tad irritable. I tell him I just went by La Cochera, and he complains that the Municipalidad de Lima is arbitrary in the way they deal with fires, how long they close down the affected market or, worse, the entire area around the burned premises.

—I agree with the shutdowns, the fines, all of it, but be consistent and fair!

He points out to the sidewalk and goes on a rant.

—Those carts out there with municipal permission, they don't touch them. Who makes a mess on the sidewalks? Not us. We have garbage bins here. It's the carts! They peel their fruit and don't have where to throw the skins away. So, they throw them right there. Two years ago, we had a rat problem. After nightfall, sometimes you see rats scurrying around on the sidewalks. But who do they fine?

The answer is implicit: vendors at El Hueco.

Roberto appears to need some peace and quiet, not my distressing questions, and despite what he just said, I feel an obligation to go back to see if Condori has made it to the office. In a few days, I'll leave Lima and won't be back until next year. I cannot miss the chance, however small, to follow up with him while he is president.

But Condori isn't there. I sit in the waiting area for another hour. I open my notebook and jot down some impressions from the morning so far. No one else comes into the office. At the hour mark, I leave. It won't be until the following August that I have a chance to speak with Condori again. He will be out of office and in big trouble, facing accusations of malfeasance and the investigations of an ad hoc committee about his dealings in Puente Piedra. He will sound worried and defeated and look older, much older. I will think, as we say in Lima

when due to misfortune a person seems to have aged ten years in one: *Se le vino el huayco.* He will look like he has been knocked down and around by a mud flood.

38

"It is an open wound," wrote the minister of health about the 2001 fire in Mesa Redonda. She was referring to the grief that had engulfed the city while in the grips of tragedy, straining to make sense of the images circulating in the media of orphans crying in the rubble, of spectral beings parading photographs of the dead and disappeared, and of charred bodies huddled inside storage rooms, melded to the goods they tried to shield. But the open wound could be said to be Mesa Redonda itself. After decades of repressive policies and interventions, merchandise seizures, fines, and business shutdowns, the labyrinthine emporium of galerías and campos feriales is nearly unchanged inside the same network of colonial-era jirones and alleys.

The open wound of the fire and of Mesa Redonda "reminds us that disastrous events are associated with disorder, poverty, overcrowding, and lack of security," the minister wrote. She uses the Spanish *hacinamiento* for overcrowding, which conveys not just a hodgepodge, disordered agglomeration but also one that transgresses bourgeois reasonableness and decorum via an excess that, in the minister's judgment, leads to the hecatombs of property and people for which Mesa Redonda and other markets are known. As in other government accounts and in the media, in the aftermath of the fires, the pragmatism, ingenuity, and grit of Lima's millions of unlicensed vendors morph into dissipation and recklessness. Vendors appear as something intimately close to the irrepressible impetus of Canetti's crowd, which brings into being a kind of countersociety in its opposition to the abstract logic of institutions. As such, the crowd's likenesses with fire—its contagiousness, insatiability, and destructive force—play out in these markets in a troubling way.

Crowds and crowdedness appeal. Canetti writes that, in a crowd, we lose our fear of being touched. This fear changes into a feeling of elation making us all equal "as though everything were happening in one and the same body." As the crowd multiplies and becomes denser, as happens during Christmas holidays and other shopping seasons at El Hueco and Mesa Redonda, the thrill easily edges into alarm and the intuition of danger. An image of the crowd in flight is built into the fantasy of being in it. "A foreboding of threatening disintegration is always alive in the crowd," Canetti writes. Moments before the 2012 fire that ruined La Cochera, a woman recalls presaging the inferno about to begin: "There were a lot of people," she told a reporter. "It was so hot, you couldn't breathe." A crowd in flight becomes "all direction, away from danger." Panic sets in and "a struggle of each against all" ensues. People push each other away like burning objects. Panic is the "disintegration of the crowd within the crowd."

Imagery of crowds—in writing, photo, or video—dominate the media's feedback loop of stories that horrify and that, paradoxically, help further attract more of the crowds that make the markets so risky but so exciting at the same time. In a 2018 newspaper article that calls Mesa Redonda a "death trap," the reporter writes that he "found hundreds of itinerant vendors that have taken over the sidewalks and pavement of Jirones Cusco and Andahuaylas." He notes that this is the spot where the 2001 fire started. "Vendors contribute to this chaos by obstructing stairwells and corridors with their products. . . . If you're thinking of going to Mesa Redonda, consider yourself warned." Plenty to give the reader pause. But the article is accompanied by the photograph of a dense and lively stream of people coursing down a colorful Jirón Puno so jam-packed with bodies and vending carts topped with eye-catching goods that one can only marvel at the power of attraction such a "death trap" exerts.

Ray Bromley notes that street vending is often deemed the "antithesis of everything modern." The crowds, disorder, and lack of hygiene and security present a contrast to the tacit ideal of speed, order, and comfort and to the gleaming aesthetics of the supermarket or shopping mall. The allusions to crudeness and savagery in the sociological literature about crowds since the nineteenth century are no longer explicit in descriptions of downtown Lima's throngs of pushcarts, peddlers, and the shoppers they attract, but these qualities still pulsate under the surface of every news coverage and analysis. The evolutionism of those reactionary descriptors isn't acceptable today because such a view of crowds sits "on the losing side of history," says William Mazzarella.

The language sits on the losing side of history, but the attraction and repulsion that crowds generate seem to have a strong staying power.

Canetti's history of crowds is strange, but it is keenly anti-evolutionist. Because of this, it affords us a glimpse into the appeal and currency of crowds as well as a better grasp of their politics and intimate relationship to the abstract, rational systems for which policy-makers such as de Soto advocate. Vendors create and shoppers seem to seek crowdedness, density, closeness to the street, saturation of color, richness of sound, a look of abundance, and the possibility, however elusive, of a just, egalitarian existence—even if this is not based on state-backed institutional arrangements, a logic of accumulation, or full enfranchisement. But this ambition is regularly thwarted by open rivalry, jealousy, self-interest, corruption, recklessness, and disaster as much as by the need to subsist in a political system that abhors street and unlicensed-market vending, that attacks them, that tolerates them (for political advantage), that coddles them (for votes), and that uses them (via bribes). What Canetti helps us appreciate is that the permanency of these vibrant but law-defying vending spaces, which no gruesome tragedy seems able to overturn, is also a sign that our fear of the powers of destruction of crowds is commensurate with our desire for them, to be in them, to be equal to others, and to obliterate distance, difference, and alienation, which can seemingly compel us to act against our interests and integrity.

Canetti disrupts the fast teleology of progress undergirding critiques of markets like El Hueco and Mesa Redonda as "the anti-thesis of everything modern." He also exposes the way that calling them marginal and precarious upholds bourgeois normative ideals and hegemonic concerns over security that are the lifeblood of such progressivism. But what are we left with if we give up progress's telos? And what do we make of the way vendors, markets, and crowds seem to self-arrogate and flaunt all the reactionary, insulting descriptors—the crude, regressive, immoderate, irrational, and dangerous qualities that crowds are accused of possessing?

What is left in the absence of the telos of progress is the reality that the crowds of Lima's markets are still a source for Peruvians' imagination of alternatives to the social order even if we don't yet know exactly what these alternatives are. "It is for the sake of . . . equality," Canetti writes, "that people become a crowd and . . . overlook anything which might detract from it." This is precisely what thirty years of failed deregulatory policy—which de Soto argued would bring order to the streets of Lima—lead us to realize: that in Canetti's words, "all demands for justice and all theories of equality ultimately derive their energy from the actual experience of equality familiar to anyone who has been part of a crowd."

39

I go down to say goodbye to Señora Viviana, Señor Vilca, and Señor Anastasio. The farewells are mostly short, to the point.

—Regrese pronto.

Of course, I'll be coming back soon. At Señora Viviana's I linger since she is unboxing an order of new bras, each neatly wrapped in its own sealed little packet. She gives me a blank sales receipt with her phone number in case I want to contact her, and I put it away in my notebook.

On my way out, I am surprised to find myself in the corridor intersection where Señora Emilia's stand used to be, looking up at the display of men's T-shirts and pants that have replaced her towels, linens, and socks. The same man who last August told me that Señora Emilia had died is there. He glances past me without the slightest air of recognition.

But maybe there is nothing to be surprised about. Señora Emilia's stand is where it all began. My conversations with Roberto took off later, after he stepped down from office. What I learned about El Hueco in the past several years has really been a mere unfolding of what Señora Emilia taught me, a fleshing out of what I learned in the first days of my research when I sat down with her at her stand. I remember that one of my first questions to her was what she thought about "informality." It was immediately clear she had given the issue a lot of thought.

—Los informales have done much for the country. What is my preference? Maybe at the beginning it is to be salaried because of the fixed income, a paycheck at the end of the month that independent workers don't have. But informality favors vendors. You make a necessity of it.

You avoid paying taxes. You work in a disorderly manner, but you don't like anyone to control you. That's my impression.

The working hours are convenient for people, she said, because they allow them to take care of their children, and workers get used to having that flexibility.

She paused before continuing:

—But every person has to collaborate with her country. You can't expect to be given and not give. The hospitals are maintained by the state. Being formal, as I am, I pay my taxes, twenty soles of the RUS.

Señora Emilia had her RUS tax ID number with SUNAT. Banks weighing lending money to El Hueco for their multi–million-dollar building project mandated that vendors have a tax ID number. The RUS was one of Fujimori's reforms implemented with de Soto's guidance. It is a flexible regimen that, according to SUNAT, fits the reality of small and microbusinesses. It frees them from having to do any bookkeeping and from being current on other taxes. It involves zero paperwork since all transactions are made verbally with a teller at the bank. In Señora Emilia's category, she could sell no more than seven thousand soles per month. Her only other obligation was to give out receipts for sales and keep copies of receipts for purchases of more than five soles. She dutifully did so, she told me.

—SUNAT can come any time and ask to see them, you know? One has to be prepared.

At the spot where I stand looking up at the new vendor's knock-off merch, the chill of crosscurrents up and down the corridors and in and out of the open ceilings picks up. It reminds me of the afternoons I sat with Señora Emilia, her thick wool sweater buttoned up to the neck, her arms crossed over her chest. Once, on one of those nippy afternoons, I offered to go up to the food court to get us a cup of hot tea only to realize I had no cash on me. I skeptically tried my debit card at the Global Net ATM booth near the market's entrance and couldn't believe my eyes when I saw the bills roll out from my bank account in New York City and had cash in hand without having to step outside of El Hueco.

I put money and debit card in my pocket and headed up to the food court to get our tea. In the grand scheme of things, this was a negligible, inconsequential transaction, a lone withdrawal and purchase of a few soles. But as I walked back to Señora Emilia's, it dawned on me that this was de Soto's whole point. For aren't individual transactions like this one, linking the very high and the very low—my reputable bank in the city of New York to the depths of El Hueco—instances of those millions of acts that, in succession and in the aggregate, deform the ideal order from within?

I expressed my surprise to Señora Emilia about El Hueco's easy access to an international banking network, and she brushed off my comment. Banks have strongly inserted themselves into the "informal sector," she told me.

—There are offers of credit everywhere. They pursue you. Before, they had a very high interest rate. But now, all they want is proof of ownership or rental of your stand, your DNI, proof of three months' payment of your RUS, and that's it. They give you your capital, and you work without stress, paying it back in monthly installments.

But if vendors fall behind, Señora Emilia said, they have to contend with the feared INFOCORP, the credit reporting agency.

As the after-work crowd of shoppers trickled in, and Señora Emilia started to look tired, I decided to leave. I told her I first wanted to buy the towel with the cute tiger cubs. She pulled an identical one out from under a folded pile, and I gave her the thirteen soles that the towel was worth, around five dollars. I bid my farewell and walked away, tucking the towel into my bag, when I noticed that Señora Emilia had neglected to give me a sales receipt. For an instant, I thought of going back and alerting her to the lapse. I wanted to tell her that for her own sake she should not let me go without the piece of paper. Remember SUNAT can come at any time! But how could I be sure it was a lapse?

Wary of coming off as condescending, I kept walking toward the exit ramp, tacitly consenting to the transaction and accepting it as yet another one of those millions of acts that add up to El Hueco's deforming influence.

40

In 2015 Lima's municipal government announced that with its support and assistance, the vendors of El Hueco had signed a contract to erect a seven-story building on their property with the aim of modernizing their establishment. The new structure would house 1,500 stores, twelve square meters each (as opposed to the current four square meters of each booth). There was more. The building would have a banks zone, a food court, offices, an auditorium for events, and two parking lots with capacity for 560 cars. The city uploaded a video to the web featuring a digital model of the exterior, a gigantic concrete and glass postmodernist structure with an adjacent tower that was, contrary to what the announcement said, not seven but ten stories high. Both mall and tower were crowned with block letters that read: "Centro Comercial El Hueco." The backdrop to the building's digital image was a luminous blue sky daubed with downy white clouds, nothing like Lima's flat-gray dome.

A seal of the Municipalidad de Lima hovered on the upper right-hand corner of the frame for the whole two plus minutes of the video's duration, as the images shifted from the building's facade to a light-drenched interior of open, spacious corridors, sleek escalators, and generous parking garages. The images were collated with scenes from the signing of the contract and clips of the speeches given by Mayor Castañeda Lossio and the president of El Hueco's cooperative, which were mainly exhortations to complete the building as the ultimate sign of vendors' success.

But the announcement was followed four days later by a media commotion that brought the construction plans to a halt as it was revealed that the design of the building was identical to—meaning it was plagiarized from—a projected mall to be built in Colombia (a fact confirmed by the Colombian construction company, stating that it would sue Lima's municipal government). Failing once more to bring the extreme space of El Hueco under control through the erection of a brick-and-mortar commercial center, the announcement was mocked online for its intention to transform Lima's main hub of piracy with a pirate design. This caused the idea of a tall, sleek building to metaphorically sink into El Hueco's quicksand of discredit.

El Hueco—hole, pit, orifice, cavity, hollow. In addition to "Formless," Bataille wrote a "critical dictionary" entry titled "Architecture." The two read as companion pieces. In the latter, he writes that architecture expresses an authority to command and prohibit. Architectural form, such as that promoted by states and religious institutions, is directed to "the multitudes and imposes silence upon them," inspiring prudence and fear. Architecture opposes "the logic and majesty of authority against all disturbing elements," Bataille states, an idea that was also behind Los Bestias's 1980s deployment of the pirate-urbanization ethos in their architectural works. The piratic element of Los Bestias opposed architecture's will to form and rejected the teleology of progress and modernization of top-down urban planning projects aimed at social integration and coherence. Los Bestias drew from architecture's lofty goals only to knock them down and strip the discipline of its future-oriented authority, affirming instead, as Biczel writes, the "mundane conditions of the appalling present" in Lima's autoconstructed barrios. Their works were homage to what Hollier describes, in reference to Bataille's formless, as "unedifying architecture" for the ways it undercuts rationality, beauty, and decorum.

Like the vendors of El Hueco, Los Bestias adopted self-deprecating titles for their works: "Des-hechos en arquitectura" (Garbage in Architecture or Architecture Undone) and "Lima: Utopía mediocre" (Mediocre Utopia). The names alluded to the material, wretched appearance of the works—as in Biczel's depiction of one that looked like a pirate ship as "ripped, twisted, flawed geometries tied with a string"—as well as amplified the group's appraisal of architecture as a discipline that was indifferent to the city's urban explosion and the plight of the majority of its residents. The words *desecho*, *deshecho*, and *mediocre*—like hueco—are never reducible to their meaning. These words compound the crude methods adopted by Los Bestias to put down architecture because of what they do, because of the effects they have on the things and places to which they are directed. This is what Bataille called the "job" or "task" of some words, which is not to describe or represent but to topple down and demote in status—the status of campos feriales like El Hueco, for example, by intensifying the reaction of disgust they engender.

When the vendors took up the moniker of hueco and when they recruited to their side the earthly powers of the plebeian Lord of Miracles to protect their specimen of pirate urbanization, they wittingly or unwittingly rejected the ideals of architecture and urban planning and affirmed, with defiance and gusto, the "conditions of the appalling present." The affective force behind the outrage that often accompanies the utterance of the market's name—bear in mind the newscaster's exclamation, "It is an authentic hole!"—makes it seem "not merely pronounced but spat out, flung in [your] face," as Hollier might say. But this is also the force I feel in my gut pulling me in every time I return to the corner of Abancay and Nicolás de Piérola and go down the ramp, now diffidently regarding the Lord of Miracles, and on the large banner tied to the ceilings I read, "Bienvenidos a El Hueco."

Indeed, welcome into the hole.

❋

Afterword

When I arrive back in Lima mid-March of 2023 for a short visit, the first thing I do is email Roberto. He likes me to let him know when I am in the city and plan to visit. It usually takes him a day or two to reply, but given I am here only for a few days, this time I don't wait. I jump on the Metropolitano and go looking for him in his stand. This is the first time I will see him since the onset of the pandemic.

Life in downtown Lima feels almost normal. Traffic along Abancay is rowdy as always, and the corner with Nicolás de Piérola buzzes with peddlers and pedestrians. I walk along the line of sidewalk-facing stands at El Hueco expecting to see the top of Roberto's cap as he bends over a box of mementos on the glass counter. But I reach the end of the block without seeing him. I turn and walk back but miss his stand again. I am confused. It is as if his stand has been swallowed by the neighboring ones. I get an eerie feeling. Something is simply not right.

Three months earlier, on the morning of December 7, 2022, I had been sitting in my living room in New York City working on this book, a Lima radio news show droning in the background, when I heard the voice of President Castillo Terrones come on in an impromptu message to the nation. My ears perked up. Frantic texting with friends and family ensued trying to figure out what was going on. Then came the familiar words, taken straight out of Fujimori's 1990 coup d'état address: "disolver temporalmente el Congreso de la República." He was shutting down Congress. It was clear Castillo felt assailed by the threats of ousting coming from Congress, but it was less clear what prompted him to stage a coup that specific morning. News outlets trained their cameras on key spots around the city and waited for the army tanks to roll down in the direction of Congress to take control of it. But that didn't happen. Instead, in the ensuing hours, the president was arrested as he and his family fled to the Mexican Embassy. Almost immediately, heated protests and road blockades erupted in Lima and in the north and south of the country. The allegation by protesters and supporters of Castillo was foul play, and the top demand was his restitution.

For weeks after Castillo's coup, pedestrian access to the intersection of Abancay and Nicolás de Piérola became difficult or impossible. On a YouTube streaming channel I watched images of one of the largest demonstrations. It was January 20, the second day of the so-called Toma de Lima, a large mobilization against Dina Boluarte, the former vice president and now the president, and in support of Castillo that was hailed as a takeover of the capital city. Caravans of people had been televised in Lima as they departed small Andean towns in Ayacucho, Puno, and other regions, putting Lima residents on edge. Through a camera stationed on the south end of Abancay, I watched as a contingent of riot police stopped a group of protesters from marching up the avenue toward Congress. Those at the front of the belligerent crowd hit the police with bats and other sticks. Three rows deep, the police lifted their shields above their heads to create a shell. The marchers hurled rocks and plastic water bottles filled with urine at them. Some of the projectiles bounced off the armor of shields. Others flew past it.

Behind the police line, the intersection was deserted. It was a rare sight that reminded me of the lockdown days of the pandemic when the Superior Courts and El Hueco were also shut, and Abancay's outbound and inbound lanes were eerily empty. On the streaming channel, I noticed that El Hueco's sign bearing the name of the market had been taken down, possibly in an effort to pass inadvertently during the violent demonstrations. As night fell, the protesters left the intersection. A reporter said that they had moved to Jirón Lampa and walked up Jirón Puno, hoping to break through the police line there in order to reach Congress. Cobblestones yanked out of the quaintly renovated old streets zoomed through the air like missiles. Much of the ire was directed at the right-wing and corrupt Congress, which the protesters and about 40 percent of Peruvians believed was behind the debacle of Castillo's government. Anger at law enforcement was close behind, given the number of abuses and unjustified killings at their hands in earlier demonstrations. The images from the lone camera suddenly turned green as if in night-vision mode. It made desolate Abancay, flanked by the unlit Courts building and a self-effacing El Hueco, look postapocalyptic.

Despite the air of normalcy everywhere else, the day I am back downtown it is clear El Hueco is experiencing a weak turnout of customers. They are still wary to enter the zone of the conflict and maneuver around riot-police formations. The new decline in business had come on the heels of a lukewarm reopening after the pandemic's long confinement period. Only half of the stands had fully reopened when the protests began, and the more than twenty thousand shoppers that before the pandemic visited El Hueco every day was estimated to have dwindled to two thousand. During the confinement, the rate of off-the-books employment in Lima had jumped to 80 percent of the labor force. Joblessness and hunger had forced young and old to ignore COVID-19–related restrictions and turn to street vending in ever higher numbers. Mesa Redonda experienced a deluge of itinerant vendors that, in contrast to the volume of customers, is still visible today.

A young woman behind a counter near where Roberto's stand used to be looks up as I walk by. The stand looks totally different, but I ask her, "Is this perhaps Señor Arispe's stand?" She returns a quiet, unfriendly stare and answers with a tiny, almost undetectable shake of the head. It is not. I go down the side entrance into the market and am near the deepest point in the hole. In a way, everything looks exactly the same as a few years ago, but the atmosphere there is also transformed. The halls are quiet and sparsely attended. At least two out of five stands are closed and padlocked. Among them are Señor Vilca's shoe and Señor Anastasio's hardware stands. I can't avoid wondering what the pandemic's impact might have been on El Hueco's old guard.

I walk over to Señora Viviana's. She is younger than Vilca and Anastasio, but I am still ecstatic to see her in her stand. Alive. She tells me that about forty cooperative members have died of COVID-19. Many of them resisted getting the vaccine, she says shaking her head. I would soon find out that Señor Martín is among the dead. As usual, Viviana is tending to her stand and her brother's across the corridor. Going up and down a drop-down ladder she moves new stock just delivered into a storage area above the stand's ceiling. I ask her, but she cannot tell me, what is going on with Vilca, Anastasio, and Roberto. She says that not only have vendors died during the pandemic, not only has the crowd of shoppers shrank and the sales plummeted, but people in general seem to have vanished.

—Before, my clients came from all over: Puno, Huánuco, Junín. They came to my stand and bought a lot, for example, during the back-to-school season.

She would have a large stock, and they would take away the bulk of it. But they don't come any more.

—I call them, and the phone rings and rings. No one answers. Will they have died, perhaps?

I walk back to Estación La Colmena. I see a short line of people holding folders and papers on the side of the Courts building. A security guard takes their DNI card and scans it before letting them in. Above the entrance, the glass has brick-size holes. The guard tells me they are from the pro-Castillo marches. Protesters hurled chunks of marble broken off the front steps at the building's glass curtain wall. Bataille says that when crowds show such animosity against buildings it is because they are "the real masters." It takes my quick exchange with the guard to notice that there is a tense calm on the stretch of sidewalk where the people have lined up to pursue bureaucratic ends, a restored, if somewhat jumpy, ordinariness. Under the stone-carved relief on the Courts building are police in riot gear, a line of about ten of them. They lean listless against the wall. I ask them for permission to take a closeup of the wall's ornamental detail, and they seem too tired or perplexed by my question to say no. I go past La Colmena to take a look at Plaza San Martín a block away. Police in riot gear are also still watching over the plaza. Boluarte cordoned it off to deprive the protesters of the symbolic political epicenter and make the protests seem disarticulated. I found out not even pedestrians are allowed to step on it.

On the bus back to Miraflores, I mull over Roberto's missing stand. He was obviously not around, and it could be that he has rearranged the interior displays. Why not? Neither is out of the question. But the two together have thrown me off. Back in my room, I am speechless when I read Roberto's email reply: He has moved with his family to Los Angeles, California.

After more than a decade wondering, every single time I set foot back in Lima, whether my main field site would still be there, I got used to the idea that El Hueco might be immovable, unassailable for economic and political reasons. I arrived every year to find little and very gradual change: new flooring, new signs for evacuation in case of a disaster, new content in some stands, and new lighting fixtures. But the market was always there. I felt a tickle of exhilaration every time. It confirmed my growing conviction of its longevity. Roberto was a crucial part of that. He was a sound businessperson, a strategist, and a trusted leader, one of the very few who could navigate the divides among vendors and between vendors and city officials. His dedication to El Hueco was total even if his faith in it was frayed. If he ever expressed a desire to leave El Hueco, I took it as a sign of momentary exasperation. Nothing more than that. Of all the changes I ever expected upon returning, it was never for Roberto to be gone, even less to have left the country.

Señor Anastasio informs me, when I finally find him in his stand a couple of days later, that many stand owners have left to the United States. He can't give me specific names. He is sitting on a short stool, dressed in cargo shorts and a bright yellow fake Adidas muscle shirt. It is an unusually informal outfit for a man his age in Lima but entirely appropriate given the El Niño–aggravated scorching March day. His reading glasses sit on the tip of his nose, and he is perusing today's issue of *La República*. Seeing me, he beams a broad smile. He throws glasses and newspaper on his messy front counter and gets up to pull up another stool for me. He says he has been away in Cuzco visiting family. He has been going there more often since his brother passed away from COVID-19 in 2021. He says this pointing across the corridor to a stand now occupied by his son, Johnny. The stand was his brother's. Anastasio lost five family members in that second wave of the pandemic, when vaccines had not yet arrived in Peru. The shortage of ICU beds and the severe deficit of liquid oxygen resulted in the largest national death rate per capita in the world. Anastasio himself got very sick and quarantined alone in the attic of his family home, certain he would also die. I tell him I had heard that the cooperative helped members through the crisis. It did, he says, but mostly just the president's friends.

—The president, he loves to brag about how much he helped associates. But he didn't help us. I begged him for oxygen for my brother. "We don't have any," he said. But I saw him helping others get oxygen. Not for my brother, though.

Anastasio says that the four hundred soles the cooperative handed its members in the early days of the crisis was an advance on yearly dividends. This was in lieu of the emergency aid the government gave to workers because that aid was only for those on payroll. He says that the cooperative payments were distributed alphabetically over the course of a few months. By the time they got to the S, the first letter of his last name, the worst part of the crisis had passed. His brother was dead and cremated. Anastasio has nothing good to say about the current president. In fact he said point blank that he is a thief. The cooperative collects dues from its members even though some drag in their payments. Besides those, it has plenty of other earnings from the bathrooms, the food court, and the many stands the cooperative rents out to vendors. The president takes advantage, he explained matter-of-factly.

—Let's say the expenses, including salaries for the staff of administrators, accountants, security guards, and janitors, is one thousand soles. If the cooperative makes two thousand, he pays all the expenses and distributes the rest among his friends.

Anastasio is certain the brick-and-mortar centro comercial on the corner of Abancay and Nicolás de Piérola will never be built.

—Never?

—There will never be a consensus—he tells me.

He is only hopeful about the piece of land in Puente Piedra and is currently serving on the committee charged with pushing the project along. At the moment, they are conducting a lottery to see where the future individual stands will be located inside the property. Only those who have paid their share of the purchase can take part in the lottery. Because it is a project built from scratch, it can materialize with however many vendors want to participate. If it is a thousand out of the fifteen hundred members, then they can design the new market with only that number in mind. He adds:

—The future is there. Very soon, in no time, there won't be anything left in the center. There will be no commerce. It is there, up north, where the consumption will be. Up there, you already have Plaza Center, with a Plaza Vea and a Tottus . . .

Plaza Center is one of the largest malls in Lima, and Plaza Vea and Tottus are two of the hypermarket chains that have sprung up in what used to be one of the peripheral new barrios in the 1980s whose population has quadrupled in size, much faster than the city's old districts.

A customer approaches and asks for a canister of some product. Anastasio gets up from his stool and enters his stand, which is packed to the brim except for a narrow lane that leads to the spot with a drop-down ladder. He pulls the ladder down and climbs up to the storage above to retrieve the product. Sitting on my stool, I see his two feet up on the ladder's top rung, and then I see them slowly coming down. During my visit, he will have two other sales: a box of nails and a replacement tube light.

The rest of the time I am at El Hueco, I can't wrap my mind around Anastasio's vision of downtown Lima's commercial world waning and disappearing. I visit with Johnny for a while. His stand is one of a growing number dedicated to selling digital technology products—chips and drives and gadgets and accessories for computers and phones of all kinds. I share what his dad has just said about the future of El Hueco being in Puente Piedra.

—Nah, he replies.

It is clear Johnny's business is thriving. By contrast, Señor Anastasio's carries only analog and mechanical hardware, and my guess is his daily sales amount to just a few soles.

Johnny tells me he knows the history of El Hueco like few others. He used to come as a boy when his father and mother both acquired stands here. This was at the very beginning, before vendors broke ground. Some had begun to build stands near the entrance while still at Mercado Central, he says, painting a more gradual and tentative picture of the market's early days. These were probably the "buildings" the Beneficencia complained about in its litigation regarding property rights. He echoes his dad's concerns about corruption at the top. He says the president is letting some friends who haven't paid their share of Puente Piedra into the lottery for the best stands at the new market. I mention Señor Condori; he also had troubles with the Puente Piedra property. Johnny gives me a raised eyebrow. I don't press the point. I later learn that Condori has been expelled from the cooperative.

Before leaving, I go by Señor Vilca's stand. His neighbor is tinkering with some garments he has displayed over Vilca's rolldown door. Vilca is in the hospital, he tells me. About ten days ago, he left the market feeling unwell. His son wants him to stay home for a while once he is discharged. I tell the neighbor to please send my *saludos* and good wishes next time he speaks with Vilca's son. I then walk down the long

and quiet corridor toward the ramp and leave the premises. If El Hueco seems unusually lifeless, outside and in Mesa Redonda the streets are teeming. Vendors have settled on both sides of the narrow jirones. But there is something amiss even with those crowds. There seem to be more vendors than shoppers.

Then, the impossible happens. I am back in New York City when I hear on the radio that Lima's new far-right mayor has declared Mesa

Redonda "zona rígida," the whole area forbidden to street vending. This means sidewalks or roads within the commercial emporium will be cleared. Seventeen thousand police and fiscal police officers as well as municipal authorities have descended on the area and blocked the access points, the newscaster explains. The update is also on *La República*'s front page, where the note says a rigid-zone ordinance for Mesa Redonda has actually been in place, although unenforced, for years. The radio news show has a special call-in and commentary block where hosts and callers discuss the drastic measure and offer their opinion on Mesa Redonda. A caller phones in:

—It is a time bomb! A time bomb! It is an area where they fry fish, fry *tequeños*. They're there with their cooking gas tanks. All cluttered. You can't even go through. It's very dangerous. It's mission impossible . . .

What dominates in Mesa Redonda, the caller finishes, is disorder and lack of authority. She doubts that the measure will last in time.

A photo in *La República* shows the unlikely, nearly surreal state of Mesa Redonda's desolate streets that morning, devoid of people and things. The host fills in while waiting for the next caller to go on the air.

—So, is it sustainable? And let's not forget it is painful for a lot of families trying to get by.

The head of citizen security at the Municipalidad de Lima later comes on for an interview. In statement after statement, which I here summarize, he falls back on trite but familiar language: We are recuperating the area. It had been invaded. Mafias have been extorting vendors occupying sidewalks and roads. It is a high-risk zone. Remember, many died in the 2001 fire. And there was another fire last year. It is extremely dangerous if there is a mass evacuation. The prior administration—well, not to blame anyone, he says—had been neglectful. He had found the area completely abandoned. Police presence might be reduced in the coming days—will not disappear, he reassures listeners.

Around that time, I speak with Roberto in LA. He says he is there because he could not do it anymore, the whole of life an uphill battle, and then the pandemic. The opportunity to leave the country arose. He made arrangements, gave up his stand, bought the tickets, and fifteen days later he was in LA. His first months the United States have been difficult, he tells me, which is to be expected for all new arrivals, but in Roberto's case it was even worse. He experienced a grave personal loss in the process. Now, in LA, he and his family are staying at his brother-in-law's. Both he and his wife work six days a week at jobs that, he says, are the kind "no one wants." But the hardest adjustments have been around routine moments one takes for granted in Lima. Once, after an overnight shift, he missed the bus home by a minute. It was 4 a.m. Exhausted and unwilling to wait an hour for the next bus, he walked home on dark and unfamiliar streets. In Lima, public transportation is dismal, but it is always available. One never feels forsaken like that, stranded so far from home.

I tell Roberto I sympathize. I tell him I cried every day my first year in the US.

—Oh, crying! We've cried rivers over here—he replies.

But he is pleased about something:

—Here in the US, you can plan ahead. You can work hard and sacrifice and actually make headway.

He is already saving money by setting aside a predictable amount every month. In Lima, nothing is predictable. Things change with the wind. In LA he has developed a five-year plan for his family to stake it out on their own. In the meantime, he has maintained his associate status at El Hueco. He still owns a stand there, the one he used to rent out. Whereas he used to receive twelve hundred soles, about $350, a month for it before the pandemic, when he left Lima, he was getting four hundred soles, a little over $100. Now the stand is without a tenant. But Roberto is convinced the centro comercial on El Hueco's site will eventually go up.

I tell him I am flying down to Lima in a couple of weeks. It is unusual for me to be back so soon, but my mother turns eighty, and, after decades of missing important family occasions, this one I am not willing to forgo. I will go to see how things are unfolding at El Hueco and Mesa Redonda now that the political turmoil has calmed down. I will report back.

—Yes, please let me know how you find everything—he says.

But as always, I think to myself, who knows what I will find. Will Mesa Redonda still be flooded with police and empty of street vendors? Will it be inundated again? Will the pandemic and the political uprising that followed Castillo Terrones's coup have made El Hueco really slip into its agonizing days, as Anastasio believes they have? Will it be booming with business again? Or will the new far-right city government have, finally, shut it down forever?

❋

Acknowledgments

I wrote earlier in this book that the first time I entered El Hueco, I felt a thrill. The place was bursting with an energy and an *empuje*, a drive, that in retrospect were familiar to me. My brother, my sister, and I were toddlers when our mother, who comes from a long line of women knitters, bought a knitting machine and put it up in our tiny attic. Photos of us at that age show us wearing pants, dresses, and skirts she made as test pieces while she taught herself to operate the device. With a small loan from a friend's father, she bought a second machine and hired a woman, Mercedes, to assist in her budding venture. The two became adept at copying and modifying styles from pictures in magazines. Soon they were selling their sweaters to a boutique on Avenida Larco, which thrived through the 1970s and 1980s when no imports were allowed in the country. In a short time, my mother and probably Mercedes, too, were the breadwinners in their families.

Some of the chaotic hustle and bustle that characterizes El Hueco and Mesa Redonda resonated with my early homelife. Up and down the three flights of stairs went cardboard boxes of yarn and large bags with pieces of sweaters to be assembled by other women in their homes. Even after she moved the small but growing business to another location, the back of my mother's station wagon was always full of deliveries of one kind or another. For as long as I can remember, she worked six days a week at this job, which demanded her full attention. At home, we continued to live and breathe the goings-on of the striving business as it navigated the turmoil of dramatic political and economic instability and a nearly always unfriendly business environment.

Growing up, I completely missed out on inheriting my mother's savvy for business, but I did pick up her knitting skills, a passion we both share. I now see that I also acquired, as if by osmosis, an interest in the risk-prone ways in which small businesses in Peru have to be run because of the red tape to which they are subjected, the need to rely on loopholes, the cat-and-mouse game this engenders, the rain of audits that pour down on them when they formalize, and, particularly back then, the country's erratic commercial and fiscal policy. While I do not think her business was ever as insecure as some of the ones at El Hueco and Mesa Redonda, I do remember that every year she seriously and anxiously considered the possibility that hers would finally tank under the weight of such unpredictability. All of this resonated with me decades later, informing my interactions with vendors and city officials and my interpretations of what I was seeing and hearing at the downtown markets featured in this book.

The book was written between June 2022 and January 2025. During this time, my mother, Marcia, generously supported me in ways that only she could have, opening her home to me during multiple research and writing stays in Lima and making sure I had everything I needed to be able to focus. Working on this manuscript in her company during quiet, breezy summer nights near the ocean is one of the highlights of my life. Thank you, Ma. Thank you also to Maday Torre Gaspar, Yorsi Sarmiento Rojas, and Julián Hinostroza Martínez for your immense help during my stays in Lima. My heartfelt gratitude also to all my friends and acquaintances at El Hueco and Mesa Redonda, for whom I have the greatest respect and admiration. Thank you for allowing me into your worlds and to share in your accomplishments and failures, your joys and sorrows.

Thank you also to Todd Ramón Ochoa, my intellectual companion in so many projects, for helping me wrestle with Bataille's latest book; to Mick Taussig for being such a wonderfully inspiring friend and mentor; to Carmen Ilizarbe for the conversations about all things to do with Peruvian politics, which became essential in my ability to follow from afar the events narrated in this book; to Patricia Oliart for her knowledge of Peruvian music, as a singer and academic, which helped clarify what I was listening to in an ecosystem in which music is vital; to Jeff Krantz for introducing me to the typologies of Bernd and Hilla Becher and other midcentury photographers who documented undervalued environments and inspired my own dabbling in photography and for, alongside Flavia Gandolfo and Ralph Bauer, guiding me in every stylistic decision, visual and narrative, I made during the manuscript phase; and to my beloved friends, family, and colleagues who have at different times shared in my work and whose own work inspire these pages: Dora King, Isaías Rojas-Pérez, María José de Abreu, Christopher Parisano, my late father Salvador Gandolfo, Ana Michell, Carlos Gandolfo, Rocío Calmet, Christopher Parkman, and Ignacio Parkman-Gandolfo.

To my editors at the University of Chicago Press: Dylan Montanari, Fabiola Enríquez Flores, and Steve LaRue as well as the anonymous reviewers of my manuscript. I couldn't have asked for better guidance. Thank you. At Wesleyan, I have been fortunate to count on the friendship and support of my colleagues Betsy Traube, Anu Sharma, and Gina Athena Ulysse (now at UC Santa Cruz) as well as on the assistance of our former student, June Labourdette, whom I thank for her sharp eye and proofreading skills. Wesleyan helped fund this book project, from its earliest days to the production process, and I am grateful for that. This work was also supported by grants from the Andrew W. Mellon Foundation and the Connecticut Rotary Foundation. Credits and my gratitude go also to the Servicio Aerofotográfico Nacional del Perú and to *Revista Caretas* for their permission to publish their stunning photos. Parts of this work, in earlier versions, have been published in the journals *Cultural Anthropology, Comparative Studies in Society and History,* and the *Journal of Latin American and Caribbean Anthropology.*

This book is dedicated to Marcia López de Romaña, Carlos Corzo Mejía, and Luis Alberto Baique, for their trust and support, which made it possible.

Notes

Note: All translations from the Spanish are mine unless otherwise indicated.

PREFACE

vii "Did You Know That Two 'Twin Towers'": Mary Sue Espíritu, "¿Sabías que en Lima se iban a construir unas 'torres gemelas,' pero en su lugar quedó El Hueco?," *La República*, September 16, 2023.

viii techniques of livelihood: Marshall Sahlins, *The New Science of the Enchanted Universe: An Anthropology of Most of Humanity* (Princeton University Press, 2022).

ix It is said to account for 78 percent of businesses: Instituto Nacional de Estadística e Informática (INEI), "Producción y empleo informal en el Perú: Cuenta satélite de la economía informal 2022," https://cdn.www.gob.pe/uploads/document/file/5634048/4990510-produccion-y-empleo-informal-en-el-peru-cuenta-satelite-de-la-economia-informal-2022%282%29.pdf; and "Situación del empleo formal e informal en Lima Metropolitana, 2022," https://cdn.www.gob.pe/uploads/document/file/5640876/4996024-boletin_situacion_empleo_formal_compressed.pdf. Note: "Informality" estimates are based on proxy metrics and thus plagued by indeterminacy.

ix a pragmatic attitude toward making a living: Hernando de Soto, *El otro sendero: La revolución informal* (Editorial El Barranco, 1986).

ix a defiant response: José Matos Mar, *Desborde popular y crisis del Estado: El nuevo rostro del Perú en la década de 1980*, Perú Problema 21 (Instituto de Estudios Peruanos, 1984).

ix the urban poor as a mass of people: Aníbal Quijano, "La formación de un universo marginal en las ciudades de América Latina," in *Antología de sociología urbana*, Colección de ciencias sociales, ed. Mario Bassols et al. (Universidad Nacional Autónoma de México, 1988), 340–65.

xi   "detours of exuberance": Georges Bataille, *The Accursed Share*, vol. 1 (Zone Books, 1988), 13.

xi   negative reciprocity: Marshall Sahlins, *On the Sociology of Primitive Exchange: Stone Age Economics* (Routledge, 1972).

CHAPTER ONE

2   "hollow": Humberto Castillo, "¿Otro Mesa Redonda? El Hueco," *La República*, January 8, 2002.

2   sinkhole: Renato Arana, "El Hueco, un espacio que subsiste desde hace 21 años en la informalidad," *La República*, July 29, 2013.

4   the kind of entrepreneurship: Hernando de Soto, *El otro sendero: La revolución informal* (Editorial El Barranco, 1986).

9   Gloria Cranmer Webster: The first quotation is from "The U'mista Cultural Center," *Massachusetts Review* 31, nos. 1/2 (1990): 133; the second is from "Dzawadi," *Anthropologica* 43, no. 1 (2001): 41.

10   U'mista Cultural Society: U'mista, "Potlatch," Living Tradition, https://umistapotlatch.ca/potlatch-eng.php.

10   "to consume": Marcel Mauss, *The Gift: The Form and Reason for Exchange in Archaic Societies* (W. W. Norton, 1990), 6.

10   reports by white settlers and officials: Christopher Bracken, *Potlatch Papers: A Colonial Case History* (University of Chicago Press, 1997).

11   "potentiality among all human groups": Holly High, "Potlatch," in *The International Encyclopedia of Anthropology*, ed. Hilary Callan and Simon Coleman (John Wiley & Sons, 2018).

11   assumes a human predisposition toward self-interest: Karl Polanyi, *The Great Transformation: The Political and Economic Origins of Our Time* (Beacon Press, 2001), 68.

11   "from becoming civilized": U'mista, "Potlatch."

11   "superabundant noneconomic motivation": Polanyi, *The Great Transformation*, 48.

11   "a society always produces more": Georges Bataille, *The Accursed Share*, vol. 1 (Zone Books, 1988), 106.

12   *dépense*: Georges Bataille, "The Notion of Expenditure," in *Visions of Excess: Selected Writings, 1927–1939*, trans. Allan Stoekl (University of Minnesota Press, 1985), 118.

14   charges of corruption were flying in every direction: "El Hueco," *Cooperativa de Servicios Especiales Mercado Central Limitada* (El Hueco newsletter), 2010.

19   "gangster rage": *Caretas*, "Jugando con fuego," no. 1458 (1997).

19   the "recuperation" of the city center: Daniella Gandolfo, *The City at Its Limits: Taboo, Transgression, and Urban Renewal in Lima* (University of Chicago Press, 2009).

20   "Refuse, offal": Friedrich Engels, "The Great Towns," in *The Condition of the Working Class in England*, ed. David McLellan (Oxford University Press, 2009), 72.

20   "tons of garbage": *Caretas*, "En el bolondrón, hermanos," no. 1465 (1997) and "Andando con Andrade," no. 1467 (1997).

20   grievances about how Lima had been clean in the past: José Guillermo Nugent, *Laberinto de la choledad* (Fundación Friedrich Ebert, 1992).

24   rival ideologies: Larissa Lomnitz, "Informal Exchange Networks in Formal Systems: A Theoretical Model," *American Anthropologist* 90 (1988): 45.

24   Los Bestias: Dorota Biczel, "Viewpoint: Self-Construction, Vernacular Materials, and Democracy Building: Los Bestias," *Buildings and Landscapes: Journal of the Vernacular Architecture Forum* 20, no. 2 (Fall 2013): 1–21.

24   Pirate urbanization: Mike Davis, *Planet of Slums* (Verso, 2006).

25   "act of taking things out of their normal or legitimate framework": AbdouMaliq Simone, "Pirate Towns: Reworking Social and Symbolic Infrastructures in Johannesburg and Douala," *Urban Studies* 43, no. 2 (2006): 357.

25   proto-Enlightenment experiments: David Graeber, *Pirate Enlightenment, or the Real Libertalia* (Farrar, Straus and Giroux, 2019).

25   "grim business": Hakim Bey, *T.A.Z.: The Temporary Autonomous Zone, Ontological Anarchy, Poetic Terrorism* (Autonomedia, 1985), 77.

25   "power to lose": Bataille, *The Accursed Share*, 1:68–77.

27   "value of the word *useful*": Bataille, "The Notion of Expenditure," 116–25.

27   "for the hell of it": Michael Taussig, "The Sun Gives Without Receiving: An Old Story," *Comparative Studies in Society and History* 37, no. 2 (1995): 392.

27   "the great and free forms of unproductive social expenditures": Bataille, "The Notion of Expenditure," 116–25.

27   *Vacation*: Roger Caillois, "Festival," in *The College of Sociology (1937–39)*, trans. Betsy Wing and ed. Denis Hollier (University of Minnesota Press, 1988).

28   "The ideal would be to give a potlatch": Mauss, *The Gift*, 151n201, 52.

28   "the danger of death is not avoided": Bataille, "The Notion of Expenditure," 119.

29   "the offering is rescued from all utility": Georges Bataille, *Theory of Religion* (Zone Books, 1992), 49.

CHAPTER TWO

38   The number of women who are street and market vendors: Lisette Aliaga Linares, "Statistics on Street Vendors and Market Traders in Metropolitan Lima and Urban Peru," Statistical Brief no. 16, WIEGO, 2017.

39   the city decided to modernize the street names: Juan Bromley, *Las viejas calles de Lima* (Fondo Editorial de la Municipalidad de Lima, 2019).

41   pleasing Odría: José Bentín Diez Canseco, *Enrique Seoane Ros: Una búsqueda de raíces peruanas* (Universidad Nacional de Ingeniería, 2014).

41   "genesis of a new man": Agrupación Espacio, "Expresión de principios de la 'Agrupación Espacio,'" *El Comercio*, May 15, 1947. This discussion is also informed by Augusto Ortiz de Zevallos, "Las ideas versus las imágenes: cuestiones al debate arquitectónico peruano," *Apuntes* 9 (1979).

43   the recently outmoded: Walter Benjamin, "Convolute J," in *The Arcades Project*, trans. H. Eiland and K. McLaughlin (Belknap Press of Harvard University Press, 1999).

43   a sensation of childhood homesickness: This section is informed by Andreas Huyssen, "Nostalgia for Ruins," *Grey Room* 23 (2006): 6–21.

45   If the documents at the archives: Beneficencia de Lima's archives, informe [report] from the Sección Judicial signed by J. L. Llosa Belaúnde and dated July 9, 1941; letter signed by Oswaldo Hercelles and dated September 7, 1959; letter signed by Antonio Icochea Aguirre and dated May 23, 1961.

45   The Beneficencia ceded pieces: Beneficencia de Lima's archives, certificates by José Jiménez Borja, November 18, 1959. Note: This transference seems to have been a protracted process involving expropriation, payment based on value, and trading for other properties.

46   Odría benefited from a spike in the global demand: Enrique Chirinos Soto, *Historia de la República, 1821–1978* (Editorial Andina, 1977); and Hernando de Soto, *El otro sendero: La revolución informal* (Editorial El Barranco, 1986).

46   a proposal to sell the property: Beneficencia de Lima's archives, memo signed by Arquitecto Fernando Bryce and dated January 26, 1966; letter signed by Teniente General FAP Eduardo Montero Rojas and dated July 13, 1978; informe [report] prepared by Flor de María Acevedo Zavala and dated August 23, 2001.

47   autoconstructed barrios: James Holston, "Autoconstruction in Working-Class Brazil," *Cultural Anthropology* 6, no. 4 (1991): 447–65.

47   "It was painful to learn": Carlos Batalla, "Los 60 años del edificio del ex-Ministerio de Educación," *El Comercio*, July 15, 2016.

48   Benjaminian dialectical image: Benjamin, "Convolute J."

48   Matos Mar: José Matos Mar, *Desborde popular y crisis del Estado: El nuevo rostro del Perú en la década de 1980*, Perú Problema 21 (Instituto de Estudios Peruanos, 1984).

48   de Soto: De Soto, *El otro sendero*, 12.

49   rebuffing of the "established order": Matos Mar, *Desborde popular*.

49   "illegal means to satisfy essentially legal objectives": De Soto, *El otro sendero*, 12.

49   "formal-legalistic" bureaucracy: Max Weber, *General Economic History*, trans. Frank H. Knight (Collier Books, 1961), 252.

49   "what is regular, predictable": Keith Hart, "Informal Economy," in *The New Palgrave: A Dictionary of Economics*, vol. 2, *E to J*, ed. John Eatwell et al. (Macmillan, 1987), 845–46.

50 "zone of penumbra": De Soto, *El otro sendero*, 12.

50 "an explosion of affective potential": Denis Hollier, *Against Architecture: The Writings of Georges Bataille* (MIT Press, 1998), 30.

52 *"Formless"*: Georges Bataille, quoted in Fred Botting and Scott Wilson, *Bataille* (Palgrave, 2001), 2.

53 $420 million: Redacción EC, "Mesa Redonda: Cierre por tres semanas provocaría pérdidas por US$420 millones," *El Comercio*, April 24, 2019.

53 "The galerías": RPP Ampliación de Noticias, interview with George Forsyth, *RPP*, April 23, 2019.

53 "mafias": Redacción RPP, "Comerciantes formales de Mesa Redonda denuncian presencia mafias que lotizan la calle," *RPP*, February 11, 2021, https://rpp.pe/lima/actualidad/coronavirus-en-peru-comerciantes-formales -de-mesa-redonda-denuncian-presencia-de-mafias-que-lotizan-la-calle -noticia-1320351?ref=rpp.

54 "the more there is of them and the denser the pile, the better": Elias Canetti *Crowds and Power* (Farrar, Straus and Giroux, 1984), 87, 76.

54 The fire's toll: Ministerio de Salud (Oficina General de Defensa Nacional), "Crónica de un incendio urbano: Mesa Redonda," 2005, https://www.gob .pe/institucion/minsa/informes-publicaciones/353453-cronica-de-un -incendio-urbano-mesa-redonda.

54 You can see it as it started: "A diez años de Mesa Redonda: El infierno estuvo en el Centro de Lima," *La República*, December 29, 2011, http://www .larepublica.pe/29-12-2011/mesa-redonda-el-infierno-estuvo-en-el-centro-de -lima (accessed November 16, 2013; no longer posted).

55 "powder keg": "Responsabilidades," *Caretas*, no. 1703 (2002).

55 "This isn't mud": Dante Castro, "Memoria del Fuego," *Caretas*, no. 1703 (2002).

55 "suicidal attempt to save them": Ministerio de Salud, "Crónica de un Incendio," 20.

55 A firefighter who finally made it to the scene: Gastón Agurto, "Lo que el fuego se llevó," *Caretas*, no. 1703 (2002).

56 the free manipulation of fire is forbidden: Roger Caillois, *Man and the Sacred*, trans. Meyer Barash (University of Illinois Press, 2001), 37.

56 "What we first learn about fire": Gaston Bachelard, *The Psychoanalysis of Fire*, trans. Alan C. M. Ross (Beacon Press, 1987), 11.

56 "a fire that utterly destroys": Georges Bataille, *The Accursed Share*, vols. 2 and 3 (Zone Books, 1993), 2:431n1.

56 "gloriously or catastrophically": Bataille, *The Accursed Share*, 1:21.

56 "hecatombs of property": Georges Bataille, "The Notion of Expenditure," in *Visions of Excess: Selected Writings, 1927–1939*, trans. Allan Stoekl (University of Minnesota Press, 1985), 122.

57 Huatica Canal: Kathrin Golda-Pongratz, "Inscripciones, incrustaciones, palimpsestos: Descifrando identidades urbanas en la Lima poscolonial contemporánea," *Anuario Americanista Europeo* 9 (2011): 87–99.

60   a special transformation phenomenon: María Rostworowski, "Pachacámac and El Señor de los Milagros," in *Native Traditions in the Postconquest World*, ed. Elizabeth Hill Boone and Tom Cummins (Dumbarton Oaks Research Library and Collection, 1998).

60   The cult of the Cristo Moreno: Susy Sánchez Rodríguez, "Un Cristo moreno 'conquista' Lima: Los arquitectos de la fama pública del Señor de los Milagros (1651–1771)," in *Etnicidad y discriminación racial en la Historia del Perú*, ed. Ana Cecilia Carrillo (Pontificia Universidad Católica del Perú, Instituto Riva-Agüero, y Banco Mundial, 2002).

60   censuses of the time: Alberto Flores Galindo, *Los rostros de la plebe* (Crítica, 1977).

62   A newspaper estimates: Redacción EC, "Cronología: 'El Hueco,' las clausuras y sanciones desde el 2002," *El Comercio*, November 19, 2014.

63   In one video: "El centro comercial El Hueco fue multado con S/. 11,400 por la MML," *Canal N*, June 27, 2014, https://canaln.pe/actualidad/centro-comercial-hueco-fue-multado-s-11400-mml -n142987?fbclid=IwY2xjawHo0QdleHRuA2FlbQIxMAABHeMfjbM _vwtc75mS7hkSN4OjbB1H3UFnUgVWqCAGLt5M1ipwyYNWegVb5A _aem_Y1yA-hfEFnK5Mou2XGTx_g (accessed July 21, 2021; no longer posted).

64   In a 2017 operation: "Policía realiza operativo contra venta de artículos piratas en El Hueco," TV Perú Noticias, November 1, 2017, https://youtu.be/JTRugs _7c9k?si=aq_7QxnP_M-bkYXG; and "Cercado: Policía realiza operativo en el centro comercial 'El Hueco,'" *Canal N*, November 1, 2017, https://canaln .pe/actualidad/cercado-policia-realiza-operativo-centro-comercial-hueco -n297618.

64   batch of alprazolam: "Incautan pastillas que eran vendidas a bandas de 'peperos' en El Hueco," *El Comercio*, September 14, 2022.

65   "*Do ut des*": Mary Douglas, foreword to Marcel Mauss, *The Gift: The Form and Reason for Exchange in Archaic Societies* (W. W. Norton, 1990), ix.

65   Bataille: All quotes are from Bataille's *The Accursed Share*, 1:69–70, except for "life grasped in its intimacy," which is from Bataille's *Theory of Religion* (Zone Books, 1994), 43–52.

67   "a succession of millions of acts": De Soto, *El otro sendero*, 3.

68   "a key distinction must be made": Miguel A. Centeno and Alejandro Portes, "The Informal Economy in the Shadow of the State," in *Out of the Shadows: Political Action and the Informal Economy in Latin America*, ed. Patricia Fernández-Kelly and Jon Shefner (Pennsylvania State University Press, 2006), 26.

69   income opportunities residents relied on: Keith Hart, "Informal Income Opportunities and Urban Employment in Ghana," *Journal of Modern African Studies* 11 (1973): 1, 61–68.

69 anti-establishment: Matos Mar, *Desborde popular.*
69 "a rationalistic economic ethic": Weber, *General Economic History,* 260.
69 economic behavior is always submerged: Karl Polanyi, *The Great Transformation: The Political and Economic Origins of Our Time* (Beacon Press, 2001), 46.
69 People experience legal regimes: Alan Smart and Filippo M. Zerilli, *Extralegality: A Companion to Urban Anthropology,* ed. Donald Nonini (Wiley-Blackwell, 2014).
69 social embeddedness of the economy: Marshall Sahlins, *On the Sociology of Primitive Exchange: Stone Age Economics* (Routledge, 1972); and Larissa Lomnitz, "Informal Exchange Networks in Formal Systems: A Theoretical Model," *American Anthropologist* 90 (1988).
69 as Lomnitz says: All quotes are from Lomnitz, *Informal Networks,* 42, 46.
70 "crowd-meaning": Canetti, *Crowds and Power,* 185.
70 "entrepreneurial reserve": De Soto, *El otro sendero,* 297.

CHAPTER THREE

74 *asociatividad*: Lisette Aliaga-Linares, *Sumas y restas: El capital social como recurso en la informalidad (Las redes de los comerciantes ambulantes de Independencia)* (Alternativa, 2002).
75 "a mythical space of shared solidarity": Manuel Marzal, "La configuración de la espiritualidad cultural y popular en un barrio marginal de la gran Lima," *La palabra y el hombre* 68 (1988): 93.
75 Nothing is left to rescue: "Galería Nicolini: Comerciantes vuelven para buscar objetos que rescatar," *Diario Correo,* August 23, 2017.
81 "secreted": Aníbal Quijano, "La constitución del 'mundo' de la marginalidad urbana," *Revista EURE* 2, no. 5 (1972): 90.
81 "la masa marginal": José Nun, "Sobrepoblación relativa, ejército industrial de reserva, y masa marginal," *Revista Latinoamericana de Sociología* 5, no. 2 (1969): 109–19.
81 "clientelism, criminality, illegal trade": José Nun, "The End of Work and the 'Marginal Mass' Thesis," *Latin American Perspectives* 27, no. 1 (2000): 25.
82 the excesses of the lumpenproletariat: Hal Draper, "The Concept of the 'Lumpenproletariat' in Marx and Engels," *Économies et sociétes* 6, no. 12 (1972).
82 refuse of all classes: Karl Marx, *The Eighteenth Brumaire of Louis Bonaparte* (International Publishers, 1972), 75.
82 gutter-proletariat: Friedrich Engels, "Preface to the Second Edition (1870)," in *The Peasant War in Germany,* trans. Moissaye J. Olgin (International Publishers, 1996), https://www.marxists.org/archive/marx/works/download/pdf/peasant-war-germany.pdf.

82   a modern form of slavery: Silvia Crespo, "Las Malvinas son asesinas: Pavoroso incendio en la galería Nicolini pone al descubierto condiciones laborales propias de esclavos en el centro de Lima," *Caretas*, no. 2494 (2017).

82   lumpenproletariat never acquired the status of a concept: Robert L. Bussard, "The 'Dangerous Class' of Marx and Engels: The Rise of the Idea of the Lumpenproletariat," *History of European Ideas* 8, no. 6 (1987): 687.

83   a politics of the lumpen: Rosalind Krauss, "'Informe' without Conclusion," *October* 78 (1996): 99.

83   "chief of the lumpenproletariat": Marx, *The Eighteenth Brumaire of Louis Bonaparte*.

87   the earthquake that hit Lima: Susy Sánchez Rodríguez, "Un Cristo moreno 'conquista' Lima: Los arquitectos de la fama pública del Señor de los Milagros (1651–1771)," in *Etnicidad y discriminación racial en la Historia del Perú*, ed. Ana Cecilia Carrillo (Pontificia Universidad Católica del Perú, Instituto Riva-Agüero, y Banco Mundial, 2002).

87   "lumpen world": Alberto Flores Galindo, *Los rostros de la plebe* (Crítica, 1977).

88   "extreme space": Sánchez Rodríguez, "Un Cristo moreno."

90   "unambiguous linear progression": Janet Roitman, *Fiscal Disobedience: An Anthropology of Economic Regulation in Central Africa* (Princeton University Press, 2005), 9.

91   "deviations, dysfunctions, or even pathologies" Janet Roitman, "The Politics of Informal Markets in Sub-Saharan Africa," *Journal of Modern African Studies* 28, no. 4 (1990): 674.

91   strong state regulations and controls are essential to capitalism: Alejandro Portes and Richard Schauffler, "Competing Perspectives on the Latin American Informal Sector," *Population and Development Review* 19, no. 1 (1993): 47.

91   "mimetic state": Hernando de Soto, *El otro sendero: La revolución informal* (Editorial El Barranco, 1986), 55–58.

91   the cohesiveness and trust: Lisette Aliaga-Linares, *Sumas y restas*.

92   "when treated individually": De Soto, *El otro sendero*, 76.

92   lumpen state, lumpen press, and lumpen empresario class: Alberto Vergara, "Lumpen-empresariado y el derrumbe del fujimorato," *Revista Quehacer* 134 (2002); and *Caretas*, "Si las elecciones fueran mañana . . . ," no. 1582 (2002).

93   organized crime: Bibiana Guardamino Soto, "Ley contra el Crimen Organizado: Advierten que PL aprobado en el Congreso excluye 59 tipos penales de la norma," *Infobae*, June 14, 2024, https//www.infobae.com/peru/2024/06/14/ley-contra-el-crimen-organizado-advierten-que-pl-aprobado-en-el-congreso-excluye-59-tipos-penales-de-la-norma.

95   "Muerte a Sulca": Redacción EC, "Dirigente baleado en el Cercado era amenazado en pintas de baño," *El Comercio*, April 28, 2015.

96   "consensus of 100% of owners and renters": "La otra cara de la galería Nicolini: Edificio será demolido y propietarios presentan nueva construcción," *La República*, April 29, 2022.

99 "critical dictionary": Georges Bataille, quoted in Fred Botting and Scott Wilson, *Bataille* (Palgrave, 2001), 2.

100 "intense and incomplete movement": Botting and Wilson, *Bataille*, 2–3.

100 "modality of insertion": Eliana Chávez O'Brien, "El empleo en los sectores populares urbanos: De marginales a informales," in *De marginales a informales*, ed. Gustavo Riofrío (DESCO, 1990), 81.

100 "The greatest hostility immigrants met": De Soto, *El otro sendero*, 11–12, 14.

101 "foreign to ideal human aspirations": Georges Bataille, "Base Materialism and Gnosticism," in *Visions of Excess: Selected Writings, 1927–1939*, trans. Allan Stoekl (University of Minnesota Press, 1985), 51.

101 "attraction-repulsion as a pair break down": Denis Hollier, preface to Georges Bataille, *Attraction and Repulsion I: Tropism, Sexuality, Laughter, and Tears*, in *The College of Sociology (1937–39)*, trans. Betsy Wing and ed. Denis Hollier (University of Minnesota Press, 1988), 103.

101 the multiplicities of vendors' economic lives: Roitman, "Politics of Informal Markets."

102 chronicle of the procession: José Carlos Mariátegui (under the pen name Juan Croniqueur), "La procesión tradicional," *La Prensa*, October 20, 1914.

104 governments and the church, in a populist move, increasingly embraced the Lord of Miracles: Julia Costilla, "Una práctica negra que ha ganado a los blancos: Símbolo, historia, y devotos en el culto al Señor de los Milagros de Lima (siglos XIX–XXI)," *Anthropologica* 36 (2016).

105 "to bless all the faithful": COOPSE El Hueco (newsletter), 2010.

105 "obviously thrilled vendors": COOPSE El Hueco, *Tu revista: Vocero de la Cooperativa de Servicios Especiales Mercado Central Ltda.* (newsletter), 2014.

105 the mystery of how this complicity: Michael Taussig, *Defacement: Public Secrecy and the Labor of the Negative* (Stanford University Press, 1999).

CHAPTER FOUR

115 Polvos Azules zips by: "Desapareció Polvos Azules," *La República*, January 2, 1993.

116 Sometime after 1941: This section is based on the Beneficencia de Lima's archives. See the notes in chapter 2, section 3.

120 *base* materialism: Georges Bataille, "Base Materialism and Gnosticism," in *Visions of Excess Selected Writings, 1927–1939*, trans. Allan Stoekl (University of Minnesota Press, 1985).

120 "all that is offensive, indestructible": Georges Bataille, "The 'Old Mole' and the Prefix Sur in the Words Surhomme [Superman] and Surrealist," in *Visions of Excess: Selected Writings, 1927–1939*, trans. Allan Stoekl (University of Minnesota Press, 1985), 32.

120   "squirrel away": Georges Bataille, *The Limit of the Useful,* ed. Cory Austin
        Knudson and Tomas Elliott (MIT Press, 2023), xli–xliii, 64.

121   "those who push the consequences of current rationalist conceptions as far
        as they will go": Georges Bataille, "The Notion of Expenditure," in *Visions
        of Excess: Selected Writings, 1927–1939,* trans. Allan Stoekl (University of
        Minnesota Press, 1985), 125–26.

121   "that 'rabble' almost unpolluted by bourgeois civilization": Mikhail Bakunin,
        The International and Karl Marx: Bakunin on Anarchism, ed. and trans. Sam
        Dolgoff (Black Rose Books, 2002).

121   "by the most underground channels": Frantz Fanon, *The Wretched of the Earth*
        (Grove Press, 1963), 81.

121   concentration in cities of this marginal mass: José Nun, "Sobrepoblación
        relativa, ejército industrial de reserva, y masa marginal," *Revista
        Latinoamericana de Sociología* 5, no. 2 (1969).

122   "*lo cholo*": Aníbal Quijano, "Lo cholo y el conflicto cultural en el Perú," in
        Dominación y cultura (Mosca Azul, 1980), 75–77.

122   "the cholo act": Urpi Montoya Uriarte, *Entre fronteras: Convivencia
        multicultural, Lima siglo XX* (Concytec and SUR, 2002), 89, 99. I note that
        in my fieldwork during the 2010s and 2020s, no one used the term *cholo*
        anymore, neither government officials nor vendors.

122   "in the bowels of the earth": Bataille, "The 'Old Mole,'" 35.

125   Then, in the summer of 2012, La Cochera burned down: This section on the
        2012 La Cochera fire and its aftermath is based on Alfa TV Noticias, "Mesa
        Redonda 'C.C. La Cochera,'" 2012, https://www.youtube.com/watch?v
        =ZGvlUZsITMw; "Bomba de tiempo: Galerías en Mesa Redonda no ofrecen
        garantías," *La República,* February 19, 2012; "Infografía: Así volvió a arder
        Mesa Redonda," *El Comercio,* February 18, 2012; "Desorden en Mesa Redonda,
        demoró la fiscalización en La Cochera," *El Comercio,* February 19, 2012;
        "Fuego arrasa con decenas de locales en Mesa Redonda y deja 20 personas
        heridas," *La República,* February 18, 2021.

126   "bad judges": DESCO, "Lima y sus jueces," *DESCO Opina—Regional,*
        Programa Urbano, June 3, 2013.

127   "land won by conquest could be distributed by the conqueror": Susan E.
        Ramírez, "Land Tenure in Early Colonial Peru: Individualizing the *Sapci,*
        'That Which Is Common to All,'" *Medieval Globe* 2, no. 2 (2016): 33–70.

127   Peru's independence in 1821: Fernando Armas Asín, "Fidelidad y realidades en
        el campo religioso: El clero y la independencia en el Perú (1820–1826)," *Análisis.
        Revista Colombiana de Humanidades,* no. 79 (July–December 2011): 243–68.

128   "time immemorial": Beneficencia de Lima's archives, informe [report]
        prepared by Flor de María Acevedo Zavala and dated August 23, 2001.

128   "transparency, luminosity, and hygiene": Dorota Biczel, "Viewpoint: Self-
        Construction, Vernacular Materials, and Democracy Building: Los Bestias,"

Buildings and Landscapes: Journal of the Vernacular Architecture Forum 20 (2): 4.

129 Odría assisted leaders of land invasions: Hernando de Soto, *El otro sendero: La revolución informal* (Editorial El Barranco, 1986), 43.

130 Mercado de la Concepción: Antonio Coello Rodríguez, "Unas notas sobre el antiguo Mercado de la Concepción, hoy Mercado Central de Lima," *Arqueología y Sociedad* 28 (2014): 367–78. For more on the history of street vending in Lima, see Fernando Iwasaki Cauti, Alonso Iván, and Enrique Ghersi, *El comercio ambulatorio en Lima* (Instituto Libertad y Democracia, 1989).

134 "It is an open wound": Ministerio de Salud (Oficina General de Defensa Nacional), "Crónica de un incendio urbano: Mesa Redonda," 2005, https://www.gob.pe/institucion/minsa/informes-publicaciones/353453-cronica-de-un-incendio-urbano-mesa-redonda.

134 countersociety: Johann P. Arnason and David Roberts, eds., *Elias Canetti's Counter-Image of Society: Crowds, Power, Transformation* (Camden House, 1996).

134 "as though everything were happening in one and the same body": Elias Canetti, *Crowds and Power* (Farrar, Straus and Giroux, 1984), 15–18.

135 "There were a lot of people": "Bomba de tiempo," *La República*.

135 "death trap": "Mesa Redonda no ha dejado de ser una trampa mortal," *Perú 21*, November 2, 2018.

135 "anti-thesis of everything modern": Ray Bromley, "Rethinking the Public Realm: On Vending, Popular Protest, and Street Politics," in *Street Economies in the Urban Global South*, ed. Karen Hansen, Walter E. Little, and B. Lynne Milgram (School for Advanced Research, 2014), 23.

135 "on the losing side of history": William Mazzarella, "The Myth of the Multitude, or Who's Afraid of the Crowd?," *Critical Inquiry* 36 (2010): 702.

136 "It is for the sake of . . . equality": Canetti, *Crowds and Power*, 26–27.

139 a seven-story building: Municipalidad de Lima, "Campo ferial 'El Hueco' se convertirá en modern centro comericial," posted on YouTube, November 19, 2015, https://youtu.be/T_4NxkWVaKQ?si=n2zA2-8R-oyK4K6u.

140 the building was identical: "¿La Municipalidad de Lima plagió proyecto de remodelación del centro comercial 'El Hueco'?," *Perú 21*, November 23, 2015.

140 a fact confirmed by the Colombian construction company: "El Hueco: Constructora colombiana tomará acciones legales por 'plagio' en diseño de remodelación," *Perú 21*, November 24, 2015.

140 a "critical dictionary" entry: Denis Hollier, *Against Architecture: The Writings of Georges Bataille* (MIT Press, 1998), 46–47.

141 "mundane conditions of the appalling present": Biczel, "Viewpoint," 16.

141 "unedifying architecture": Hollier, *Against Architecture*, xi.

141 "ripped, twisted, flawed geometries": Biczel, "Viewpoint," 1.

141 "not merely pronounced but spat out": Hollier, *Against Architecture*, 30.

AFTERWORD

153   "zona rígida": "Rotativa del aire," RPP, May 15, 2023.

153   rigid-zone ordinance for Mesa Redonda: Ricardo Mc Cubbin, "MML declara a Mesa Redonda y Mercado Central como zonas rígidas, pero ya lo eran hace más de 20 años," *La República*, May 14, 2023.

Figure Credits

All photos by Daniella Gandolfo with the following exceptions:

9   Servicio Aerofotográfico Nacional. 1978. Intersection of Avenidas Abancay and Nicolás de Piérola, Lima.

21   *Revista Caretas.* 1997. Jirón Huallaga, Lima.

26   *Top left quadrant,* photograph by Andrea Urrutia. 2010. La Cochera, Mesa Redonda.

40   Seoane sketch in Bentín Diez Canseco. 2014. Photograph by Daniella Gandolfo.

117   *Top,* Leonce Angrand. 1847. Santa Teresa Church, Lima. *Bottom,* Postcard, Convento Santa Teresa, Lima.

131   Postcard, Mercado de la Concepción, Lima.

Index

* 9 7 8 0 2 2 6 8 4 3 3 9 1 *